ACTION PHILOSOPHERS!

The lives and thoughts of history's A-list brain trust

VOLUME TWO

by Fred Van Lente and Ryan Dunlavey

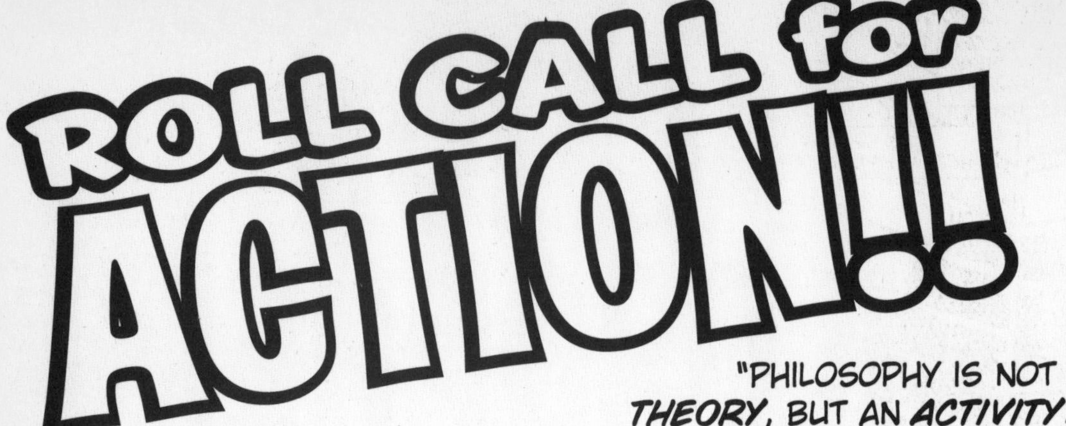

"PHILOSOPHY IS NOT A *THEORY*, BUT AN *ACTIVITY*."
--LUDWIG WITTGENSTEIN, *TRACTATUS LOGICO-PHILOSOPHICUS*

ACTION PHILOSOPHERS GIANT-SIZE THING VOL. 2 IS PUBLISHED BY EVIL TWIN COMICS, 262 FIFTH AVENUE, 2ND FLOOR, BROOKLYN NY, 11215. THE MATERIAL IN THIS BOOK ORIGINALLY APPEARED IN PERIODICAL FORM IN *ACTION PHILOSOPHERS #4-6*. FIRST PRINTING: DECEMBER 2006. PRINTED IN CANADA.

ISBN-10: 0-9778329-1-0
ISBN-13: 978-0-9778329-1-0

A SPECTER IS HAUNTING EUROPE--
THE SPECTER OF ACTION PHILOSOPHER #10:
KARL MARX
WHEN I WAS A KID, THERE WAS ONE THING ABOUT THE WAY THE WORLD WORKED THAT I NEVER ENTIRELY UNDERSTOOD.
OD DUKE
I MEAN, BY THIS POINT I HAD FIGURED OUT THAT THE WHOLE POINT OF LIVING WAS TO MAKE MONEY.
SPECIAL
27.
MILK
BUT, IF THAT WAS THE CASE...
WRITERS OF THE WORLD! UNITE BEHIND FRED VAN LENTE! DOWN WITH EFFETE BOURGEOIS "ARTISTE" RYAN DUNLAVEY!

"A COMMODITY IS, IN THE FIRST PLACE, AN OBJECT MADE OUTSIDE OF US, A THING THAT BY ITS PROPERTIES SATISFIES HUMAN WANTS OF SOME SORT OR ANOTHER."
-- DAS KAPITAL VOL. 1 (1867)

BUTCHER
FINE MEATS
THE NATURE OF SUCH WANTS, WHETHER, FOR INSTANCE, THEY SPRING FROM THE STOMACH OR FROM FANCY, MAKE NO DIFFERENCE!
PHONEY
YOUR DISTINCTION BETWEEN 'NECESSITY' AND 'LUXURY' IS A DANGEROUS FALLACY, FREDDY!
AW.

THE UTILITY OF A THING MAKES IT A USE-VALUE!
USE-VALUES BECOME A REALITY ONLY BY USE OR CONSUMPTION... THEY ARE, IN ADDITION, THE MATERIAL DEPOSITORIES OF EXCHANGE-VALUE.

BUT THERE IS AN EVEN MORE IMPORTANT IMMATERIAL FACTOR THAT DIFFERENTIATES COMMODITIES FROM EACH OTHER.
A USEFUL ARTICLE HAS VALUE ONLY BECAUSE HUMAN LABOR HAS BEEN EMBODIED OR MATERIALIZED IN IT!

THE MAGNITUDE OF THIS VALUE IS MEASURED BY THE QUANTITY OF THE LABOR CONTAINED IN THE ARTICLE!
QUANTITY OF LABOR IS MEASURED BY DURATION --TIME!

AFTER ALL, IT TAKES MORE TIME TO SEW A SUIT THAN IT DOES TO WEAVE CLOTH -- AND LESS TIME THAN THAT TO PICK COTTON!
AND THE EXCHANGE VALUES OF THOSE ITEMS REFLECT THAT DIFFERENCE!
00:03
01:69
25:42
$
$$
$$$

"CAPITALISTS" ARE PEOPLE WHO BENEFIT FROM THE EXCHANGE, NOT THE PRODUCTION OF COMMODITIES. THEY ARE THE BOURGEOISIE...THE MIDDLE CLASSES WHO WERE MONEYLENDERS AND USURERS IN MEDIEVAL TIMES...

... AND IN OUR MODERN ERA, THEY'RE THE FACTORY OWNERS AND LANDLORDS WHO CONTROL THE MEANS OF PRODUCING COMMODITIES.

THE KEY TO CREATING SURPLUS VALUE IS TO MAKE SURE
THAT WAGES REMAIN ***LESS*** THAN THE EXCHANGE VALUE OF THE COMMODITIES
THAT THE WORKERS PRODUCE.

EVEN ***BETTER***, SINCE YOUR WORKERS DON'T DIRECTLY REAP THE ***BENEFITS*** OF THEIR OWN LABOR, THEY'LL SUFFER FROM ***ALIENATION***.

FEELS LIKE I'VE SPENT MY WHOLE ***LIFE*** AT THIS CRUMMY JOB...

...BUT ***TODAY*** WAS MY ***FIRST DAY***!

TO COMPENSATE, THEY'LL GORGE THEMSELVES ON ***COMMODITIES*** WITH EVERY DIME THEY MAKE!

WHOEVER DIES WITH THE MOST TOYS ***WINS***! BWHAHAHA!!

HE'S NOT JUST THE ***PRODUCER***, HE'S ALSO THE ***CONSUMER...***

AND ***I*** POCKET THE DIFFERENCE IN THE FORM OF ***SURPLUS VALUE***! HEH-HEH!

GEEZ ... WORKERS EXCHANGE THEIR LABOR-TIME FOR WAGES... WHICH THEY GIVE ***BACK*** TO THE CAPITALIST SO THEY CAN ***BUY*** THE VERY COMMODITIES THEY ***PRODUCE***!

WHAT A ***VICIOUS CYCLE***! IS THERE ANY WAY IT CAN BE ***BROKEN***, MR. MARX?

ACTUALLY, I CAN THINK OF ***SIXTY*** WAYS, FREDDY!

M-60, THAT IS.

KLIK-KLAK!

LET'S ***DO*** THIS THING.

UH...

...WHAT THING WOULD ***THAT*** BE, MR. MARX?

*: K.M. & F. ENGELS, *MANIFESTO OF THE COMMUNIST PARTY* (1847)

*: DITTO

GOSH KNOWS I DIDN'T START OUT THAT WAY, FREDDY! I WAS BORN IN PRUSSIA IN 1818. MY DAD WAS A LAWYER, AND I WENT TO SCHOOL TO STUDY LAW, BUT I GOT BITTEN BY THE PHILOSOPHY BUG, INSTEAD...
GRENADE ME, FREDDY.
FLASHBANG OR INCENDIARY?
INCENDIARY.

THANKS.
I WAS A STUDENT OF HEGEL'S, BUT I REJECTED HIS IDEALISTIC DIALECTIC FOR A MATERIALLY-DETERMINED THEORY OF HISTORY.
IDEAS ARE ALL WELL AND GOOD, BUT I HUNGERED TO CHANGE THE WORLD, NOT MERELY INTERPRET IT...

...SO I TURNED TO JOURNALISM. I WORKED FOR A BUNCH OF LEFTIST WORKERS' PAPERS. THAT GOT ME KICKED OUT OF PRUSSIA ... THEN FRANCE, WHEN THOSE TWO COUNTRIES BECAME ALLIES ...
CHINK!

... THEN I WOUND UP IN LONDON, WHERE THE COMMUNIST LEAGUE ASKED ME AND MY COLLEAGUE FRIEDRICH ENGELS TO WRITE A MANIFESTO ON THEIR BEHALF.
TOSS!
THAT WAS IN 1847. I BECAME A BIG WHEEL IN THE MOVEMENT AFTER THAT. I TRAVELED ALL OVER EUROPE, ORGANIZING WORKERS' PARTIES...

BWHOOM!
...AND EVERYWHERE, I SAW THE SAME POVERTY AND MISERY AMONG THE WORKERS -- THE SAME FORCED IGNORANCE! LIKE WE WROTE IN THE MANIFESTO:
"THE DEVELOPMENT OF MODERN INDUSTRY CUTS FROM UNDER ITS FEET THE VERY FOUNDATION ON WHICH THE BOURGEOISIE PRODUCES AND APPROPRIATES PRODUCTS."

AAAAAH! AAAAAAH!
"WHAT THE BOURGEOISIE PRODUCES, ABOVE ALL, IS ITS OWN GRAVE-DIGGERS."
"ITS FALL AND THE VICTORY OF THE PROLETARIAT ARE EQUALLY INEVITABLE."

B-BUT, I MEAN, THE OVERTHROW OF ALL SOCIAL CONDITIONS? IS THAT REALLY NECESSARY?
Y-YOU KNOW, SINCE YOU WERE ALIVE, A LOT OF POSITIVE THINGS HAVE HAPPENED IN CAPITALIST SOCIETY --
POW
-- LABOR UNIONS, SOCIALIZED MEDICINE, MINIMUM WAGE, CHILD LABOR LAWS...

REFORMIST DRIVEL!
BOURGEOIS "SOCIALIST" COMPROMISE!
BAND-AIDS ON A CANCER PATIENT!

NOBODY LISTENS! I TOLD THEM COMMUNISM WOULD ONLY BE POSSIBLE IN A GLOBAL REVOLUTION!
THE WORLD CANNOT EXIST PART CAPITALIST AND PART COMMUNIST--IN A HEAD-TO-HEAD MATCH-UP, CAPITALISM WILL ALWAYS WIN!
BULGARIA
WHY?
POLAND
UKRAINE S.R.
BELARUS S.R.
USSR

"BECAUSE CAPITALISM IS NOTHING IF NOT DUCTILE! FROM TIME TO TIME GROUPS COME ALONG WHO FANCY THEMSELVES REVOLUTIONARY--"
LOOK OUT, HETERO-HEGEMONY! HERE COMES QUEER THEORY!
POST-COLONIALISM IS GONNA KNOCK YOU ON YOUR PASTY WHITE IMPERIALIST ASS, CRACKER!
WE REJECT THE GENDERED SUBJECT IMPOSED ON US BY PHALLO-CENTRISM!

"--BUT CAPITALISM APPEASES WOULD-BE REFORMERS -- ABSORBS THEM INTO ITSELF -- SEDUCING ONE-TIME SOCIAL PARIAHS INTO BECOMING JUST ANOTHER DEMOGRAPHIC FOR ITS COMMODITIES!"
FIERCE MONTHLY
AFRICA
SEX in the CITY

FOR CAPITALISM IS NOT FUNDAMENTALLY *WHITE* -- OR *STRAIGHT* -- OR *MALE*!
REVOLUTION RECORDS
MARX BREW
COFFEE ROASTERS
LENIN LIT
OPEN
RED or DEAD ROAST
IT HAS NO QUALMS ABOUT "EMBRACING" *ANY* IDEOLOGY, SO LONG AS ITS *OWN* EXISTENCE IS PERPETUATED!

AND IF THE BOURGEOISIE CANNOT EXPLOIT THEIR *OWN* COUNTRYMEN FOR SURPLUS VALUE--
MADE IN CHINA
--THEY'LL JUST MOVE JOBS *OVERSEAS* IN ORDER TO FIND *NEW* VICTIMS!

THOUGH CAPITALISM APPEASED THE *FIRST WORLD*'S LABOR MOVEMENT WITH REFORMS LIKE MINIMUM WAGE...
LENIN LIT
...THE VAST MAJORITY OF THE COMMODITIES PRODUCED FOR YOUR *"LIBERAL"* REPUBLICS...
...ARE PRODUCED *FAR* FROM THE MALLS AND SUBURBS WHERE THEY'RE SOLD!

THERE THE SITUATION OF THE 21ST CENTURY PROLETARIAT IS NO DIFFERENT THAN THE EUROPEAN FACTORY WORKERS OF *MY* DAY!
WAGES MEASURED IN *PENNIES*--UNSAFE CONDITIONS--INADEQUATE HEALTH CARE AND EDUCATION--*NO* HOPE FOR SOCIAL ADVANCEMENT--
BUT WHEN THE THIRD WORLD STARTS DEMANDING *ITS* RIGHTS --
--AND THE CAPITALISTS RUN OUT OF PEOPLE WILLING TO BE EXPLOITED--
--THEN THE *TRUE* COMMUNIST ERA WILL BEGIN!

"ONCE THE WORKERS SEIZE THE MEANS OF PRODUCTION, SURPLUS VALUE WILL BE ***ELIMINATED!***
THE BASIS OF THE ***COMMUNIST*** ECONOMY IS:"

"From each according to his abilities, to each according to his needs."

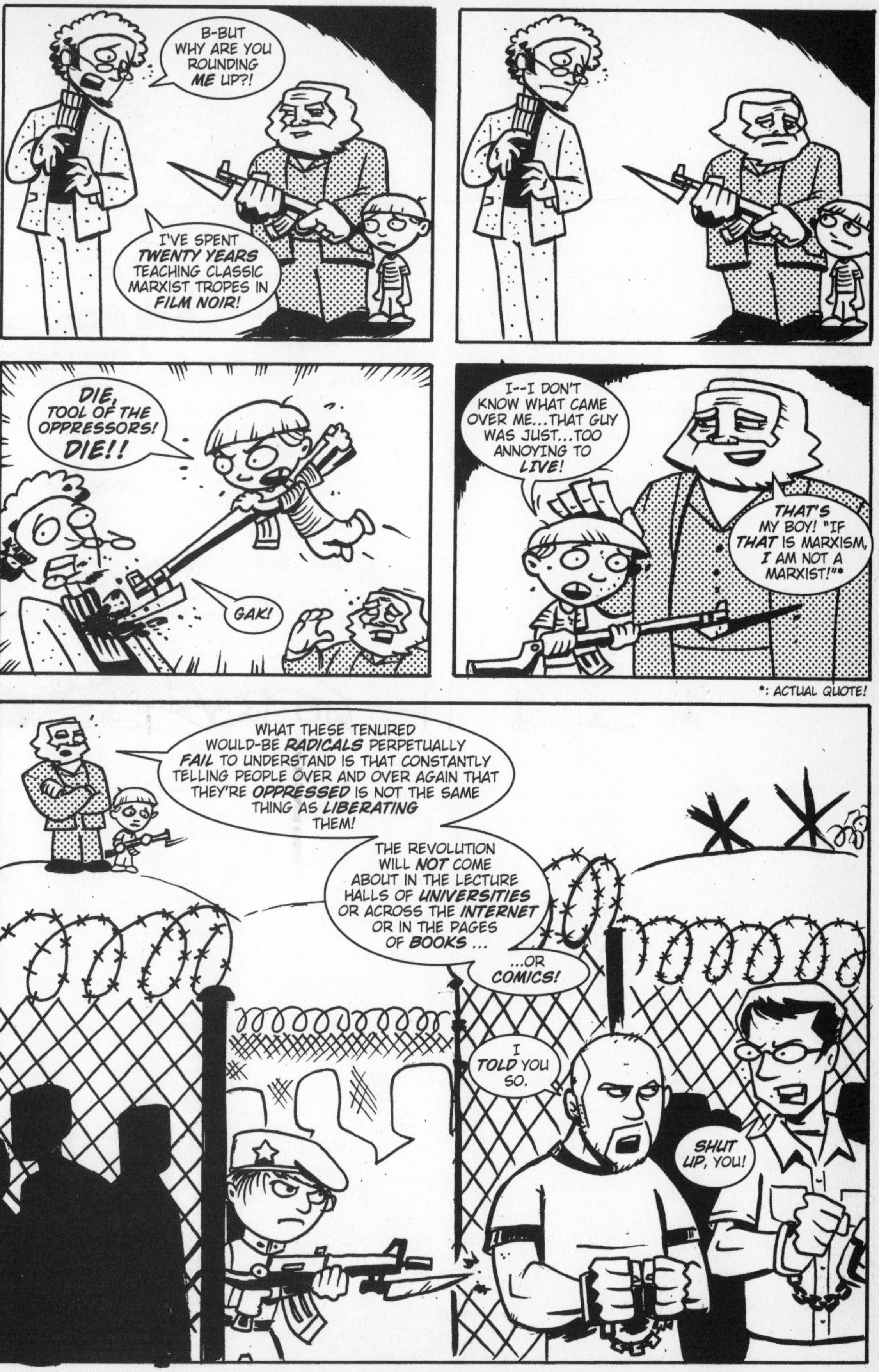

*: ACTUAL QUOTE!

WHAT THESE TENURED WOULD-BE RADICALS PERPETUALLY FAIL TO UNDERSTAND IS THAT CONSTANTLY TELLING PEOPLE OVER AND OVER AGAIN THAT THEY'RE OPPRESSED IS NOT THE SAME THING AS LIBERATING THEM!

THE REVOLUTION WILL NOT COME ABOUT IN THE LECTURE HALLS OF UNIVERSITIES OR ACROSS THE INTERNET OR IN THE PAGES OF BOOKS ...

...OR COMICS!

I TOLD YOU SO.

SHUT UP, YOU!

"THE WRITER MAY VERY WELL SERVE A MOVEMENT OF HISTORY AS ITS MOUTHPIECE, BUT HE CANNOT OF COURSE CREATE IT."
ONLY THE MASSES CAN LIBERATE THE MASSES!
SOUNDS LIKE A PRETTY TALL ORDER, MR. MARX!

"SO IT IS, FREDDY! WAGE-SLAVES ARE NO LESS TRAPPED BY THEIR MATERIAL CONDITIONS THAN THE CHATTEL OF PRE-CAPITALIST ERAS!"
"THEIR PAY IS KEPT AS LOW AS POSSIBLE (TO MAXIMIZE SURPLUS VALUE), SO THEY CAN ONLY AFFORD WHAT THEY NEED TO SURVIVE--"

"--AND PRODUCE MORE LABORERS FOR CAPITALIST EXPLOITATION! (EVER NOTICE HOW THE POORER AND LESS EDUCATED A FAMILY IS, THE MORE KIDS IT PUMPS OUT?)"
FOXY
"SO THE NECESSITIES OF LIFE MUST REMAIN CHEAP AND PLENTIFUL SO WORKERS CAN BUY THEM EVEN WITH THEIR PITIFUL WAGES..."

BLAM! BLAM! BLAM!
...AND THAT'S WHY MILK IS CHEAPER THAN GOLD!
SO WHAT DO YOU THINK, FREDDY?
I--I THINK I WANT MY MOMMY...

WHY, SURE--SHE'S RIGHT OVER THERE!
SAY-- YOU NEVER MENTIONED SHE WORKED IN A BANK!
WAAAAA!!
ENDINGS OF THE WORLD! UNITE!

1527:
I CALL THIS MEETING OF THE COUNCIL OF THE TEN OF THE FLORENTINE REPUBLIC TO ORDER!
THE FIRST ITEM ON THE AGENDA IS THE REINSTATEMENT OF OUR FORMER SECRETARY...
...ACTION PHILOSOPHER #11...
NICCOLÒ MACHIAVELLI!
this tale hath been told byest:
federico di lente III, duke scripturio & Ryan "Il fuzzino" of the erieshire dunlaveys, first earl of the comely doodles

NO POINT IN ***HANGING AROUND***, OLD MAN--THE ***TEN*** TAKE A WHILE TO DECIDE ***ANYTHING***.

RETURN TO YOUR MASTER-- ***WE'LL*** TELL YOU WHICH WAY THE VOTE ***SWINGS***.

TH-THANK YOU, KIND ***CLERKS.*** >KOF!< I--I LIVE TO ***SERVE***-- >KOF!<

IS IT ***TRUE***, FORTUNATO? WILL THE LEGENDARY ***MACHIAVELLI*** RETURN AT LAST TO GUIDE THE STATECRAFT OF FLORENCE?

WHY ***NOT***? AFTER ALL, HE RECEIVED HIS ***FIRST*** POSITION WHEN THE MEDICI* GOT TOSSED OUT THE ***LAST*** TIME!

1494:

THE GREATEST OF THE LINE, LORENZO ***"THE MAGINIFICENT"*** DE' MEDICI, BEAUTIFIED THE CITY WITH PAINTING AND SCULPTURE...

(*: THE ***MEDICI*** FAMILY, BANKERS TO THE ***POPE***, HAD RULED FLORENCE SINCE THE BEGINNING OF THE FIFTEENTH CENTURY.

...BUT AFTER LORENZO'S DEATH HIS WORTHLESS SON ***PIERO*** TOOK OVER.

WHEN THE FRENCH INVADED ITALY TO CLAIM THE THRONE OF NAPLES, PIERO ***FLED*** THE CITY AND THE ***FIRST*** FLORENTINE REPUBLIC WAS FOUNDED IN HIS ABSENCE!

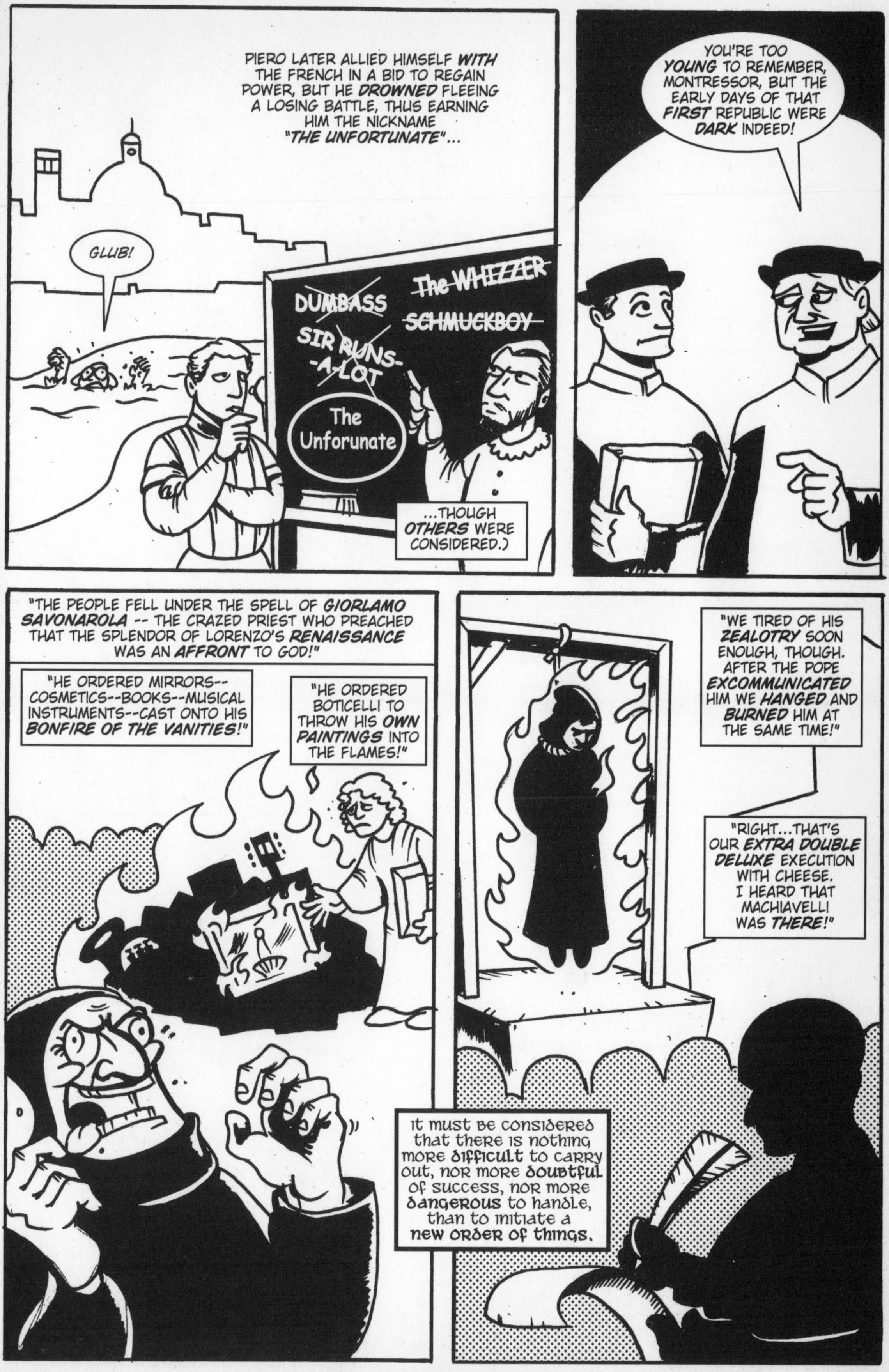

"THE PEOPLE FELL UNDER THE SPELL OF GIORLAMO SAVONAROLA -- THE CRAZED PRIEST WHO PREACHED THAT THE SPLENDOR OF LORENZO'S RENAISSANCE WAS AN AFFRONT TO GOD!"

"HE ORDERED MIRRORS--COSMETICS--BOOKS--MUSICAL INSTRUMENTS--CAST ONTO HIS BONFIRE OF THE VANITIES!"

"HE ORDERED BOTICELLI TO THROW HIS OWN PAINTINGS INTO THE FLAMES!"

"WE TIRED OF HIS ZEALOTRY SOON ENOUGH, THOUGH. AFTER THE POPE EXCOMMUNICATED HIM WE HANGED AND BURNED HIM AT THE SAME TIME!"

"RIGHT...THAT'S OUR EXTRA DOUBLE DELUXE EXECUTION WITH CHEESE. I HEARD THAT MACHIAVELLI WAS THERE!"

It must be considered that there is nothing more difficult to carry out, nor more doubtful of success, nor more dangerous to handle, than to initiate a new order of things.

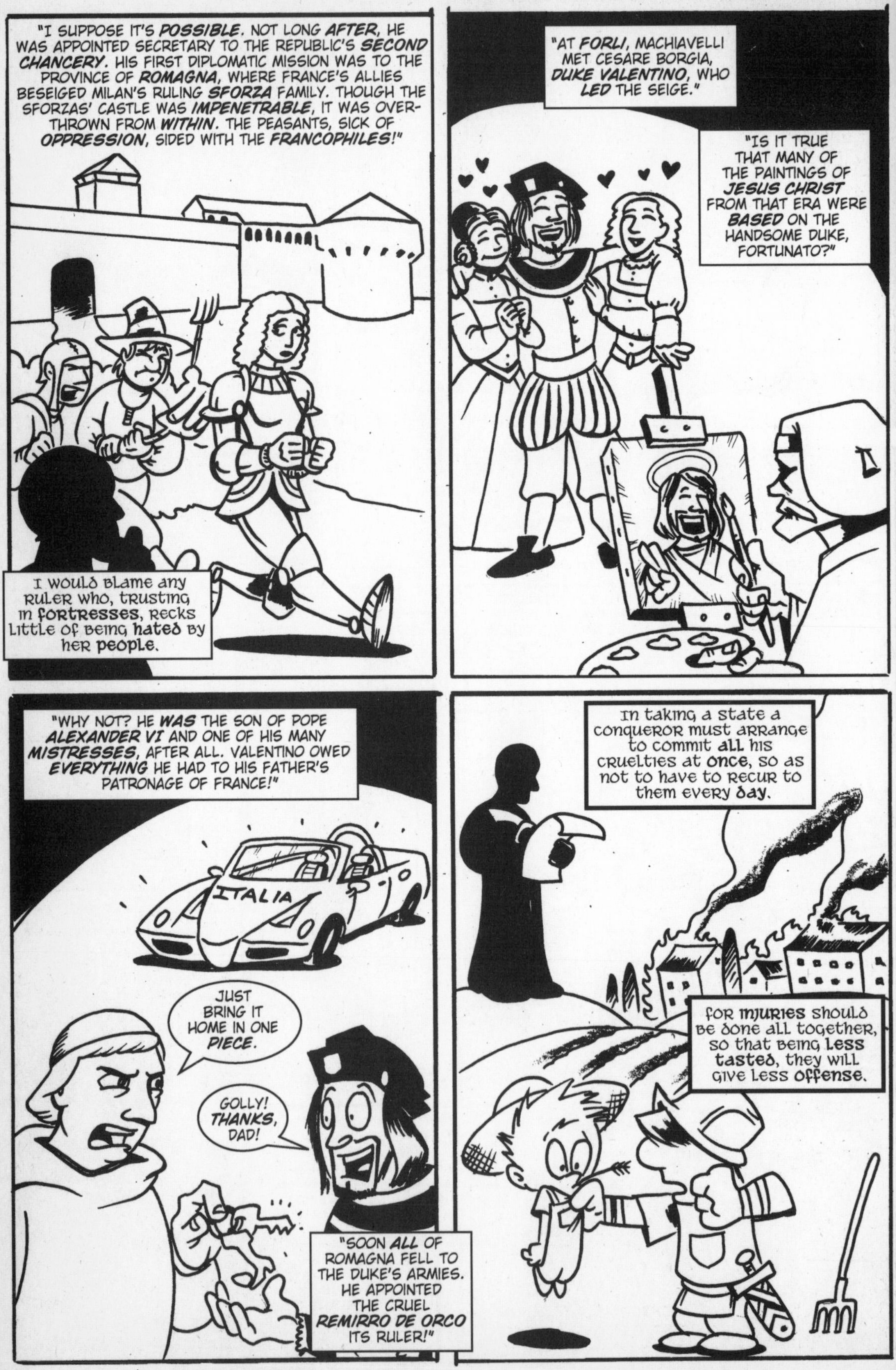

"WHY NOT? HE ***WAS*** THE SON OF POPE ***ALEXANDER VI*** AND ONE OF HIS MANY ***MISTRESSES***, AFTER ALL. VALENTINO OWED ***EVERYTHING*** HE HAD TO HIS FATHER'S PATRONAGE OF FRANCE!"

ITALIA

JUST BRING IT HOME IN ONE ***PIECE***.

GOLLY! ***THANKS***, DAD!

"SOON ***ALL*** OF ROMAGNA FELL TO THE DUKE'S ARMIES. HE APPOINTED THE CRUEL ***REMIRRO DE ORCO*** ITS RULER!"

In taking a state a conqueror must arrange to commit **all** his cruelties at **once**, so as not to have to recur to them every **day**.

For **injuries** should be done all together, so that being **less tasted**, they will give less **offense**.

this man (Remirro), in a short time, was highly successful in rendering the country orderly and united:
REMIRRO TERRORIZES POOR FARMERS AND IMPRISONS THE PEASANTRY FOR NO GOOD CAUSE, DUKE VALENTINO!
HMMM... YOU DON'T SAY... THAT'S AWFUL... TSK!
whereupon the duke, not deeming such excessive authority expedient, lest it become hateful, resolved to show that if any cruelty had taken place, it was not by his orders, but through the harsh discipline of his minister.
Duke's Orders: Terrorize Imprison

there are many who think therefore that a wise prince ought, when he has the chance, to foment astutely some enmity, so that by suppressing it...
WHA-- WHAT I DO WRONG? GAK!
...he will augment his greatness.

"WHO KNOWS HOW FAR VALENTINO COULD HAVE CLIMBED, HAD HIS FATHER NOT DIED SO SUDDENLY?"
"SCANDALMONGERS SAY THE POPE PLANNED TO POISON A CARDINAL, BUT THE WILY CLERIC SWITCHED THEIR SWEETMEAT BOXES, SO ALEXANDER'S OWN TREACHERY DID HIM IN!"

"GOOD RIDDANCE, I SAY. THE REPUBLIC SENT MACHIAVELLI TO ROME TO MONITOR THE ELECTION OF THE NEW POPE."
GO POPE!
"DUKE VALENTINO, SUFFERING FROM A FEVER, WAS MANIPULATED INTO ALLOWING AN ENEMY OF THE BORGIAS BE ELECTED POPE JULIUS II!"

"IF VALENTINO THOUGHT JULIUS WOULD BE GRATEFUL, HE WAS IN FOR A NASTY SURPRISE!"
whoever thinks that in high personages new benefits cause old offenses to be forgotten, makes a great mistake.
the duke erred in his choice and it was the cause of his ultimate ruin.

"WITH VALENTINO *IMPRISONED*, ROMAGNA TURNED TO *VENICE* FOR MILITARY PROTECTION. BUT JULIUS II WOULDN'T STAND FOR THAT -- HE *PERSONALLY* LED PAPAL ARMIES AGAINST THEM!"
BATTLEPOPE
"MACHIAVELLI WAS MUCH *IMPRESSED* BY THE BOLDNESS WITH WHICH THE NEW POPE CONQUERED *BOLOGNA*:"

Fortune is a **woman**, and it is necessary, if you wish to **master** her, to conquer her by **force**.
POPE OF THE BEACH
It can be seen that she lets herself be overcom by the **bold** rather than by those who proceed **coldly**.
777

"THE POPE FORMED A PACT WITH SPAIN, FRANCE AND THE *HOLY ROMAN EMPIRE* TO OPPOSE THE VENETIANS!"
LEAGUE of CAMBRAI

"BUT ONCE VENICE WAS BROUGHT TO THE PAPAL HEEL, JULIUS SWITCHED ALLIES *AND* AIMS -- JOINING *WITH* THE CITY TO DRIVE THE FRENCH OUT OF ITALY!"
NO FRENCHIEZ ALLOWD
SACRE BLEU!
If men were all **good**, it would be good to keep faith with them; but as they are **bad**, and would not observe faith with **you**, you are not bound to keep faith with **them**.

"I BELIEVE MACHIAVELLI WAS IN VIENNA THROUGH 1508, SERVING AS ENVOY TO HOLY ROMAN EMPEROR MAXMILIAN I. HE WAS LESS THAN IMPRESSED:"
a secret man, he does not communicate his designs to anyone or take any advice...
PLANS

...but as on putting them into effect they begin to be known and discovered, they begin to be opposed by those he has about him, and he is easily diverted from his purpose.

a prince ought always to take counsel, but only when he wishes, not when others wish...
...he ought to be a great asker, and a patient hearer of the truth about those things of which he has inquired.
LISTEN
ACT

we have in our own day ferdinand, the present king of spain.
he had recourse to a pious cruelty...
ACT
UK
FRANCE
SPAIN

...driving out the moors (and the jews) from his kingdom and despoiling them.
these and other acts have kept his subjects' minds uncertain and astonished, so that they have left no time for men to settle down and plot against him.

"IT TOOK ALL OF MACHIAVELLI AND HIS FELLOW MINISTERS' DIPLOMATIC SKILLS TO KEEP FLORENCE OUT OF THE ITALIAN WARS. BUT HE LEARNED THE HARD WAY:"
Irresolute princes, to avoid present dangers, usually follow the way of neutrality, and are mostly ruined by it.

"THE POPE COULD NO LONGER RISK THE POSSIBILITY THAT FLORENCE MIGHT ALLY WITH HIS ENEMIES. IN 1512, FERDINAND'S ARMIES OCCUPIED THE CITY, AND THEN, BY PAPAL DECREE..."
HONEY, I'M HOME!
"...JULIUS RETURNED THE MEDICIS TO POWER! GUILIANO, PIERO'S BROTHER, BECAME THE CITY'S NEW DUKE!"

"A MEDICI GOON SQUAD SOON ARRESTED TWO YOUNG REPUBLICAN CONSPIRATORS WITH A LIST OF PEOPLE THEY THOUGHT MIGHT BE SYMPATHETIC TO AN OVERTHROW OF PAPAL CONTROL!"

?

"GUESS WHO'S NAME THEY FOUND ON IT?"
PHILLIP BERADUCCI
CHARLES CIPPRIANO
NICCOLO-MACHIAVELLI
WILLIAM PAGANO
ANTHONY MARANO

"-GASP!- DID MACHIAVELLI NAME NAMES?"
"HOW COULD HE? HE HAD NO IDEA HOW HIS NAME GOT ON THE LIST IN THE FIRST PLACE!"

"HIS LIFE WAS ***SPARED***-- BUT THE MEDICI BANISHED HIM TO A FARM IN THE ***SUBURBS***, HIS GOVERNMENT POSITION FOREVER ***LOST!***"

"->*FEH!*<- SOME ***MERCY!*** TO EXILE ONE SUCH AS ***NICCOLO*** FROM THE HALLS OF POWER ... THEY MIGHT AS WELL HAVE CUT OFF HIS ***AIR SUPPLY!***"

STILL, HE FOUND A WAY TO KEEP BUSY IN HIS ***LIBRARY***:

on the threshold I slip of my day's clothes with their mud and dirt, put on my curial robes, and enter the ancient **courts** of the men of **old**.

I am not ashamed to address them and **ask** them the reasons for their action, and they **reply** considerately; and for two hours I **forget** all my cares.

and since **dante** says that we can never **attain** knowledge unless we **retain** what we hear, I have noted down the capital I have accumulated from their conversation and composed a **little book**...

"HE DEDICATED HIS WORK TO PIERO'S SON ***LORENZO*** IN AN ATTEMPT TO WIN THE FAVOR OF THE MEDICIS AND RECLAIM HIS POSITION!"

"IT CONTAINED THE ***SUM TOTAL*** OF MACHIAVELLI'S STUDY OF ANCIENT LORE, COMBINED WITH HIS ***DECADES*** OF EXPERIENCE IN GOVERNMENT SERVICE!"

the herein-mentioned things, if **prudently** observed, make a **new** prince seem **ancient**, and render him at once more secure and firmer in the state than if he had been established there of **old**.

IL PRINCIPE

my intention being to write something of **use** to those who understand, it appears to me more proper to go to the real **truth** of the matter than to its imagination.

how we live is so far removed from how we **ought** to live, that he who abandons what **is** done for what **ought** to be done, will rather learn how to bring about his own **ruin** than his preservation.

a man who wishes to make a profession of goodness in **everything** must necessarily come to grief among so many who are **not** good.

therefore it is necessary for a **prince**, who wishes to **maintain** himself...

...the **end** justifies the **means**.

"THE STUPID BRAT NEVER READ THE COPY OF THE PRINCE MACHIAVELLI PRESENTED TO HIM--"
"--IF HE HAD, MAYBE HIS FAMILY WOULDN'T HAVE BEEN EXILED AGAIN!"
CHUCK!

"THE PEOPLE OF FLORENCE TURNED AGAINST THE POPE WHEN FOREIGN TROOPS --HIS OWN ALLIES-- SACKED ROME!"
"WE REPUBLICANS ARE BACK ON TOP AGAIN!"

SINCE THEN, THE PRINCE HAS BECOME RENOWNED ACROSS EUROPE--EVEN I HAVE WHOLE CHAPTERS MEMORIZED!
WITH MACHIAVELLI AGAIN AT THE HELM OF FLORENCE'S STATE-CRAFT, NO DOUBT THE REPUBLIC'S SECURITY IS ASSURED--
SSSHH!! SOUNDS LIKE DEBATE IS WINDING DOWN--

SO IT'S UNANIMOUS THEN!

THANKS TO OUR FORMER SECRETARY'S CYNICAL SCREED, THE VERY WORD "MACHIAVELLIAN" HAS BECOME A SYNONYM FOR RUTHLESS DUPLICITY!
WE CANNOT HAVE SUCH A PERSON WORKING FOR US!

THE CITIZENS OF FLORENCE MUST KNOW THEIR GOVERNMENT IS RULED BY FAITH, CHARITY AND RELIGION!
SIGNOR MACHIAVELLI'S PETITION IS REJECTED!

BU-BUT... MACHIAVELLI DID NOTHING MORE THAN TELL THE TRUTH ABOUT HOW POWER WAS WIELDED IN HIS TIMES--
EXACTLY! ONE OF THE WORST THINGS YOU CAN DO IN GOVERNMENT IS BE SMARTER THAN YOUR SUPERIORS!
HE FORGOT ONE OF HIS OWN MAXIMS--

It is not, therefore, necessary for a prince to have faith, charity and religion...
THE NEXT BILL WOULD ALLOW US TO DEDUCT OUR MISTRESSES AS BUSINESS EXPENSES! ALL THOSE IN FAVOR--?
AYE!
AYE!
AYE!
AYE!
...but it is necessary to seem to have them.

GUESS WE'D BETTER FIND THAT SERVANT SO HE CAN GIVE HIS MASTER THE BAD NEWS...
UH-OH! SEE WHERE ALL THOSE PEOPLE ARE GATHERED--ISN'T THAT THE ADDRESS HE GAVE US?

WHAT HAS HAPPENED, SIGNORA?
>SOB!< POOR SIGNOR MACHIAVELLI--THE FEVER FELLED HIM AS SOON AS HE GOT BACK FROM THE PALAZZO VECCHIO!

I DIDN'T EVEN RECOGNIZE HIM -- THE TORTURE HAS AGED HIM SO, THE POOR PAPER-PUSHER!
MACHIAVELLI DIED WITHOUT EVER LEARNING THAT HIS BELOVED FLORENTINE REPUBLIC HAD OVERWHELMINGLY REFUSED TO RETURN HIM TO OFFICE.
GASP! THAT BROKEN-DOWN OLD FARMER... HE WAS THE FEARED MACHIAVELLI?!
AND "HONEST MEN" HAVE USED HIS NAME AS A PEJORATIVE EVER SINCE!
IL FINITO

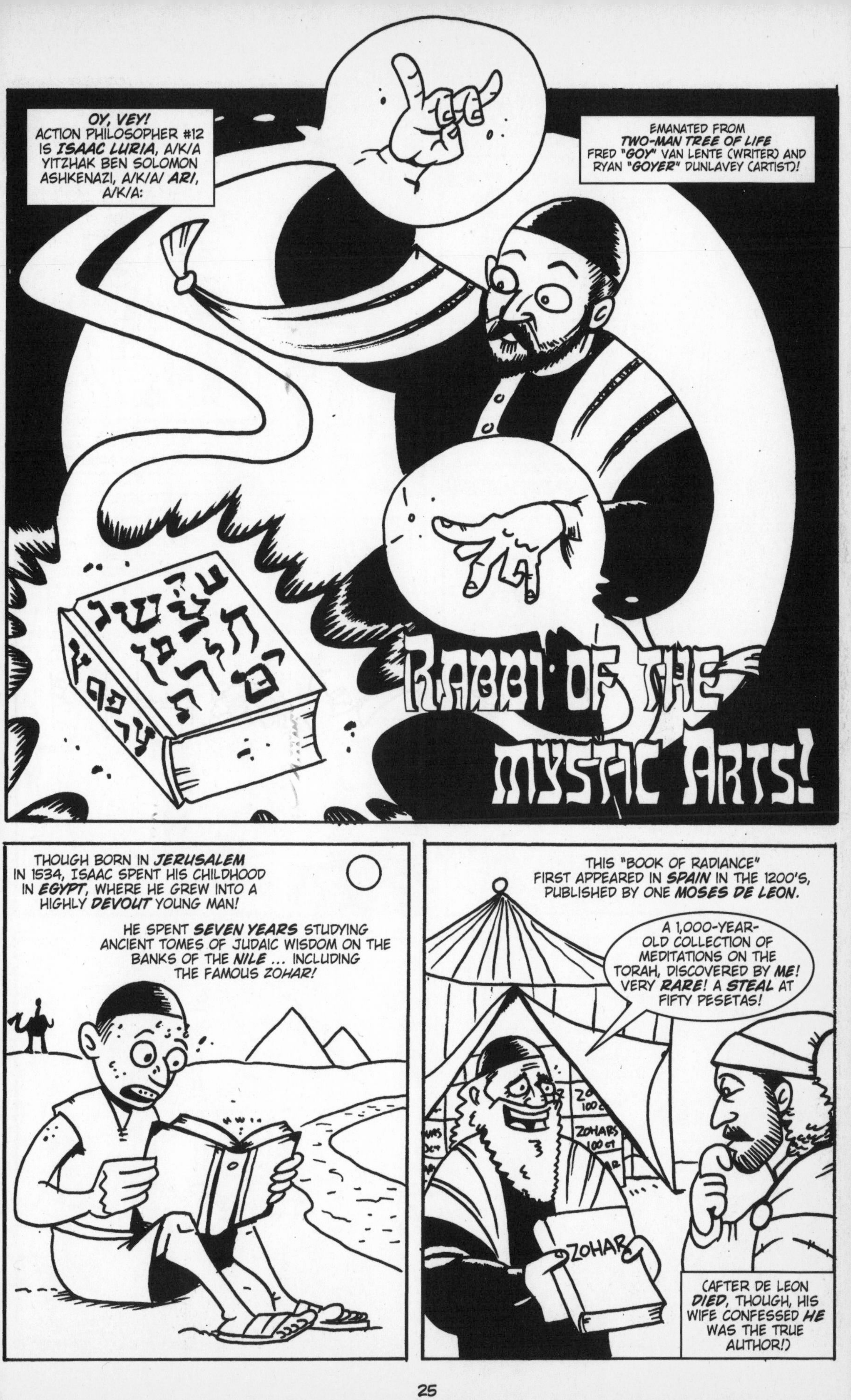

OY, VEY! ACTION PHILOSOPHER #12 IS ***ISAAC LURIA***, A/K/A YITZHAK BEN SOLOMON ASHKENAZI, A/K/A/ ***ARI***, A/K/A:

EMANATED FROM ***TWO-MAN TREE OF LIFE*** FRED "***GOY***" VAN LENTE (WRITER) AND RYAN "***GOYER***" DUNLAVEY (ARTIST)!

RABBI OF THE MYSTIC ARTS!

THOUGH BORN IN ***JERUSALEM*** IN 1534, ISAAC SPENT HIS CHILDHOOD IN ***EGYPT***, WHERE HE GREW INTO A HIGHLY ***DEVOUT*** YOUNG MAN!

HE SPENT ***SEVEN YEARS*** STUDYING ANCIENT TOMES OF JUDAIC WISDOM ON THE BANKS OF THE ***NILE*** ... INCLUDING THE FAMOUS *ZOHAR!*

THIS "BOOK OF RADIANCE" FIRST APPEARED IN ***SPAIN*** IN THE 1200'S, PUBLISHED BY ONE ***MOSES DE LEON***.

(AFTER DE LEON ***DIED***, THOUGH, HIS WIFE CONFESSED ***HE*** WAS THE TRUE AUTHOR!)

LIKE THE PLACEBO THAT ACTUALLY CURES THE PATIENT, HOWEVER, DE LEON'S ZOHAR SPARKED THE SCHOOL OF JEWISH MYSTICAL THOUGHT KNOWN AS THE KABBALAH, WHICH MEANS...
TRADITIOOOOON! TRADITION!
6th Grade FIDDLER on the ROOF
...OR, MORE LITERALLY, "THAT WHICH IS RECEIVED."

KABBALISTS, FOLLOWING THE ZOHAR, REFER TO THE JEWISH GOD AS EIN SOF--
I THINK GOD'S DOWN THERE SOMEWHERE... -GULP!-
--AN ESSENTIALLY UNKNOWABLE "INFINITE" FROM WHICH ALL CREATION EMANATES.

CONTEMPLATING EIN SOF ALONG THE NILE, ISAAC HAD A VISION OF THE PROPHET ELIJAH...
THE TIME FOR STUDYING IS OVER! YOU MUST NOW GO OUT INTO THE WORLD, AND SHARE WHAT YOU'VE LEARNED WITH GOD'S CHOSEN PEOPLE!
BUT FIRST... TAKE A SHOWER, WILLYA? PEE-YEW!

THE LURIAS DECAMPED FOR ISRAEL, SPECIFICALLY SAFED, A SMALL TOWN IN THE MOUNTAINS OF GAILILEE AND A HOTBED OF KABBALIST STUDY.
ISAAC'S STUDENTS CALLED HIM ARI-- A HEBREW ACRONYM FOR "OUR MASTER RABBI ISAAC" THAT ALSO MEANS "LION"--
-- SO THEY CALLED THEMSELVES THE "CUBS!"

THIS TREE OF LIFE IS THE COSMIC FLOWCHART BY WHICH EIN SOF EMANATES REALITY--
--I CALL EACH STAGE OF THAT PROCESS A SEFIRAH, OR "ENUMERATION!"
כתר
בינה
חכמה
גבורה
חסד
תפארת
הוד
נצח
יסוד
מלכות

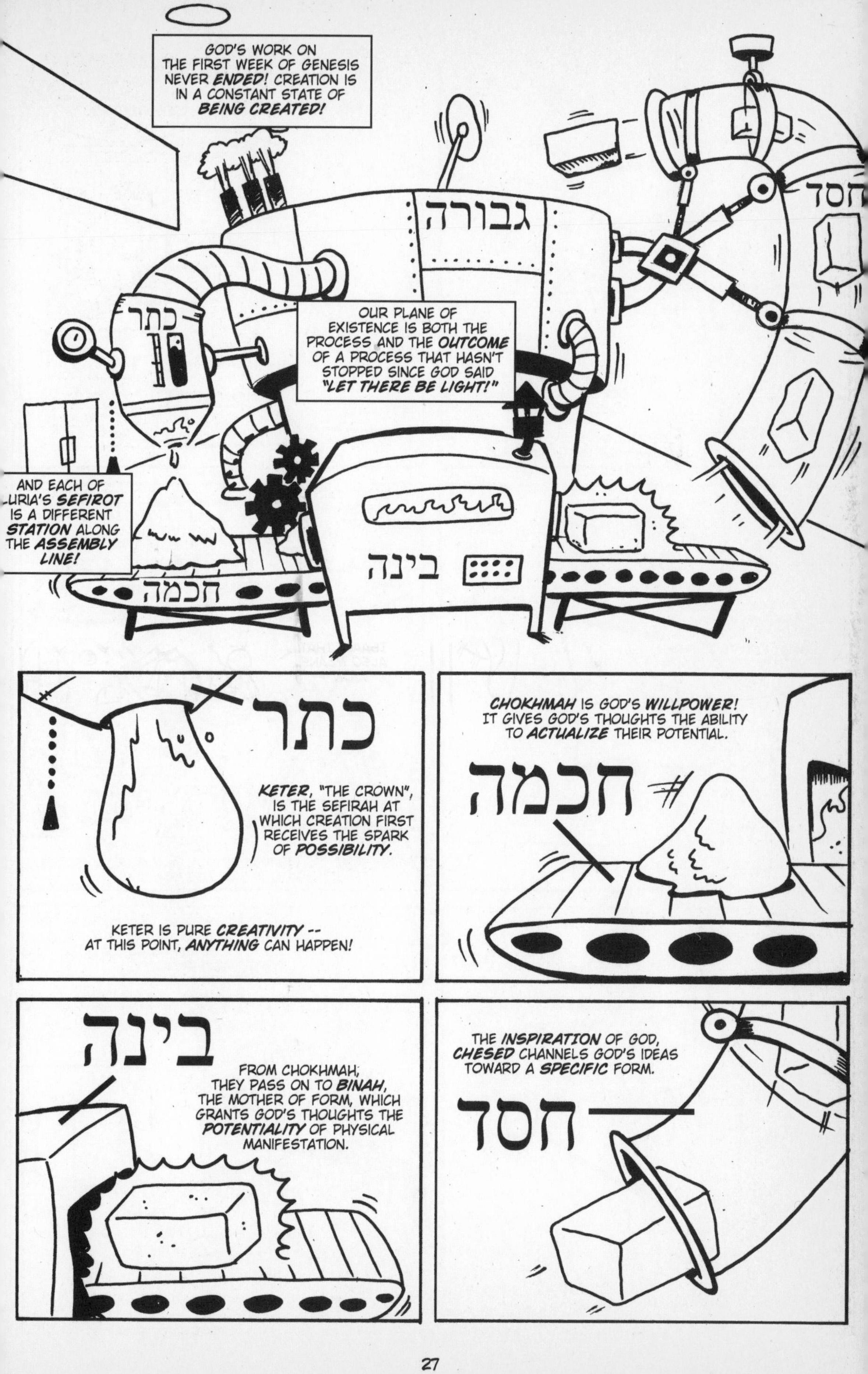

GOD'S WORK ON THE FIRST WEEK OF GENESIS NEVER *ENDED!* CREATION IS IN A CONSTANT STATE OF ***BEING CREATED!***

גבורה

חסד

כתר

OUR PLANE OF EXISTENCE IS BOTH THE PROCESS AND THE ***OUTCOME*** OF A PROCESS THAT HASN'T STOPPED SINCE GOD SAID ***"LET THERE BE LIGHT!"***

AND EACH OF LURIA'S ***SEFIROT*** IS A DIFFERENT ***STATION*** ALONG THE ***ASSEMBLY LINE!***

בינה

חכמה

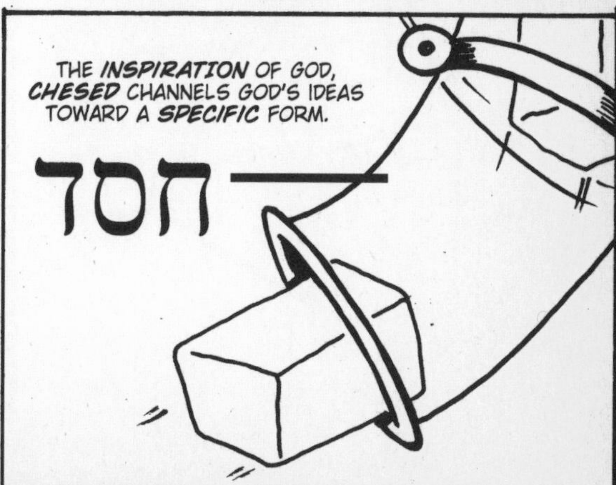

גבורה
BEFORE ANYTHING *NEW* CAN BE CREATED, THE *OLD* MUST BE DONE AWAY WITH.
GEVURAH IS THE GREAT *DESTROYER* OF THE SEFIROT...

... WHILE *TIPHERETH* IS THE GREAT *BALANCER* ...
THE *RATIONAL* PART OF THE DIVINE MIND!
100%
תפארת

BY PASSING THROUGH *NETZACH*, GOD'S IDEAS PICK UP THE QUALITY OF *DESIRE* -- THE URGE TO *CREATE* -- THAT *MOTIVATES* CREATION!
נצח

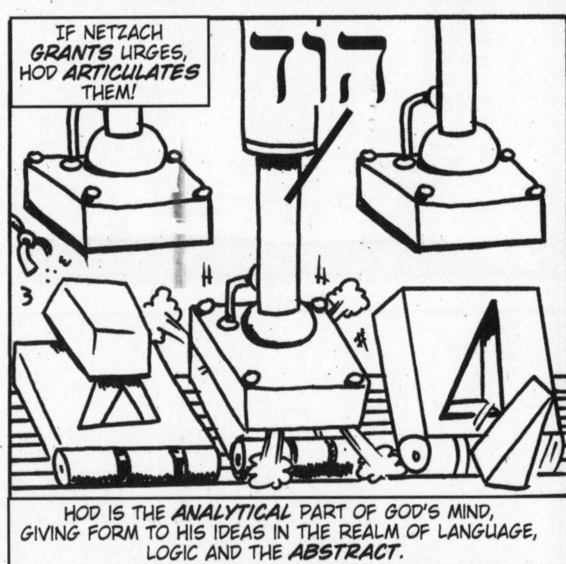
IF NETZACH *GRANTS* URGES, HOD *ARTICULATES* THEM!
הוד
HOD IS THE *ANALYTICAL* PART OF GOD'S MIND, GIVING FORM TO HIS IDEAS IN THE REALM OF LANGUAGE, LOGIC AND THE *ABSTRACT*.

YESOD SPECIFIES THE PLATONIC FORMS THAT GOD'S IDEAS MAY TAKE; BUT THEY ARE SPECIFIC-*GENERIC*, AS OPPOSED TO SPECIFIC-*INDIVIDUAL*.
יסוד
now 100% More REAL !!!
REALITY

ALSO KNOWN AS "THE KINGDOM", *MALKUTH* IS THE "OUTPUT TRAY" OF THE TREE OF LIFE, THE *FINAL* MANIFESTATION OF GOD'S THOUGHTS INTO *CORPOREAL REALITY*.
"THE WORD MADE FLESH," AS THE BIBLE SAYS, AND MALKUTH ENCOMPASSES THE FLESH OF THE *ENTIRE PHYSICAL UNIVERSE*!
REALITY
מלכות

THE HEBREW TEXT OF THE TORAH IS THE ***ASSEMBLY LANGUAGE*** FOR REALITY! SOME KABBALISTS HOLD THAT IF ALL ITS LETTERS WERE TO BE ***REARRANGED***, THE SECRETS OF THE UNIVERSE WOULD BE ***UNLOCKED***... THE MOST ***SIGNIFICANT*** BEING THE ***TRUE NAME OF GOD***. IT IS CONSIDERED ***BLASPHEMOUS*** TO SPEAK THIS NAME ALOUD, SO IT IS REPRESENTED IN MOST BIBLES AS JUST ***FOUR CONSONANTS***...

YHWH

... THE SO-CALLED ***"TETRAGRAMMATON"***! IN HEBREW, ***"YHWH"*** LOOKS LIKE THE THIRD PERSON SINGULAR IMPERFECT OF THE VERB "TO BE" ... SO THE JEWISH GOD IS A ***LIVING*** GOD, ALWAYS IN THE PROCESS OF ***BECOMING***!

THIS IS BECAUSE THE TREE OF LIFE IS A **TWO-WAY** CONDUIT TO THE INFINITE.
JUST AS WHAT GOD DOES AFFECTS **US**, WHAT **WE** DO AFFECTS **HIM**, AND, BY EXTENSION, **REALITY**!

BY CLEAVING **TOWARDS** GOD, DOING **GOOD WORKS**, AND LEADING A PIOUS LIFE, A HUMAN BEING **HELPS** GOD, AND THEREFORE CREATION, INTO A MORE FULLY **REALIZED** STATE.
SNIFF, SNIFF! WE'RE **GETTING** THERE...

CONVERSELY, EVIL, **SELFISH** ACTIONS IMPEDE THE FLOW OF CREATION, AND ARE **DETRIMENTAL** TO GOD.
>ERRK!< I'M GETTIN' **VERKLEMPT** HERE! STAY OUTTA YOUR MOTHER'S PURSE, SHLOMO!
OY!

LURIA HIMSELF WAS SAID TO POSSESS MANY **MYSTICAL POWERS** DERIVING FROM HIS ABILITY TO INFLUENCE THE **FLOW** OF REALITY.
"THE ELEMENTS OF **TIME, SPACE,** AND **MOTION** ARE MERELY AN EXPRESSION OF THE **LIMITATIONS** IMPOSED BY THE PHYSICAL BODY ON THE **SOUL**."
"WHEN THE **SOUL** HAS SWAY OVER THE **BODY**, THESE LIMITING FACTORS **CEASE TO EXIST**."

"LET US NOW PROCEED TO **JERUSALEM**, FOR OUR **PHYSICAL BODIES** HAVE LOST THEIR INFLUENCE OVER OUR **SOULS**!"
BEAM ME UP, ISAAC!

LURIA DIED IN 1572 AT THE AGE OF 38 WITHOUT HAVING WRITTEN ANYTHING DOWN.
WAIT! DON'T KICK OFF JUST YET--LET ME GET DOWN THAT LAST BIT OF WISDOM--
GAK!
DAMMIT!
BUT THE CUBS CAPTURED AS MANY OF HIS TEACHINGS AS THEY COULD IN THE SIX VOLUMES OF THE TREE OF LIFE, WHICH SOON SPREAD THROUGHOUT THE JEWISH WORLD.

WHILE THE OTHER MONOTHEISTIC RELIGIONS HAVE HAD A TENDENCY TO NEGLECT OR PERSECUTE THEIR OWN MYSTICAL TRADITIONS, MAINSTREAM JUDIASM HAS ALWAYS AT LEAST TOLERATED THE KABBALAH.
GNOSTICISM
SUFISM

NOT THAT THERE HAVEN'T BEEN A FEW BUMPS IN THE ROAD.
YHWH!
A LURIANIC KABBALIST NAMED SABBATAI ZEVI CAUSED A MAJOR SCHISM BETWEEN RABBINICAL JUDIASM AND THE JEWISH MASSES IN THE 1600'S BY PROCLAIMING HIMSELF THE MESSIAH.

EVEN AFTER ZEVI CONVERTED TO ISLAM (OUCH), THE REBELLIOUS SPIRIT HE ENGENDERED PERSISTED, CULMINATING IN THE FOUNDATION OF THE HASIDIC MOVEMENT AROUND 1740...
PRAISE BE TO ALLAH!
FEH! WHO NEEDS 'IM?
...USING LITURGY DEVELOPED BY LURIA TO CREATE A LESS SCHOLARSHIP-BOUND JUDIASM THAT (THEY FELT) CONNECTED BETTER TO THE MASSES' SPIRITUAL NEEDS!

THE TREE OF LIFE INFLUENCED ***CHRISTIAN*** THOUGHT AS WELL...PARTICULARLY AMONG ***ALCHEMISTS*** WHO WERE TRYING TO INFLUENCE CREATION IN RATHER ***MATERIAL*** WAYS...

NOPE. STILL ***LEAD.***

YOU KNOW, WE REALLY ***SUCK*** AT THIS.

AND, OF COURSE, THE RECENT FASCINATION OF MANY ***CELEBRITIES*** WITH THE KABBALAH, SPEARHEADED BY ***MADONNA***, HAS BEEN WELL-PUBLICIZED.

TABLOIDS REPORTED THAT POP STAR ***BRITNEY SPEARS*** PLANNED TO GIVE BIRTH TO HER FIRST CHILD IN A POOL FILLED WITH ***ONE THOUSAND*** ONE-LITER BOTTLES OF SPECIALLY BLESSED ***"KABBALAH WATER!"*** (AT A PRICE TAG OF ***$3,800!***)

HIT ME BABY

POP!

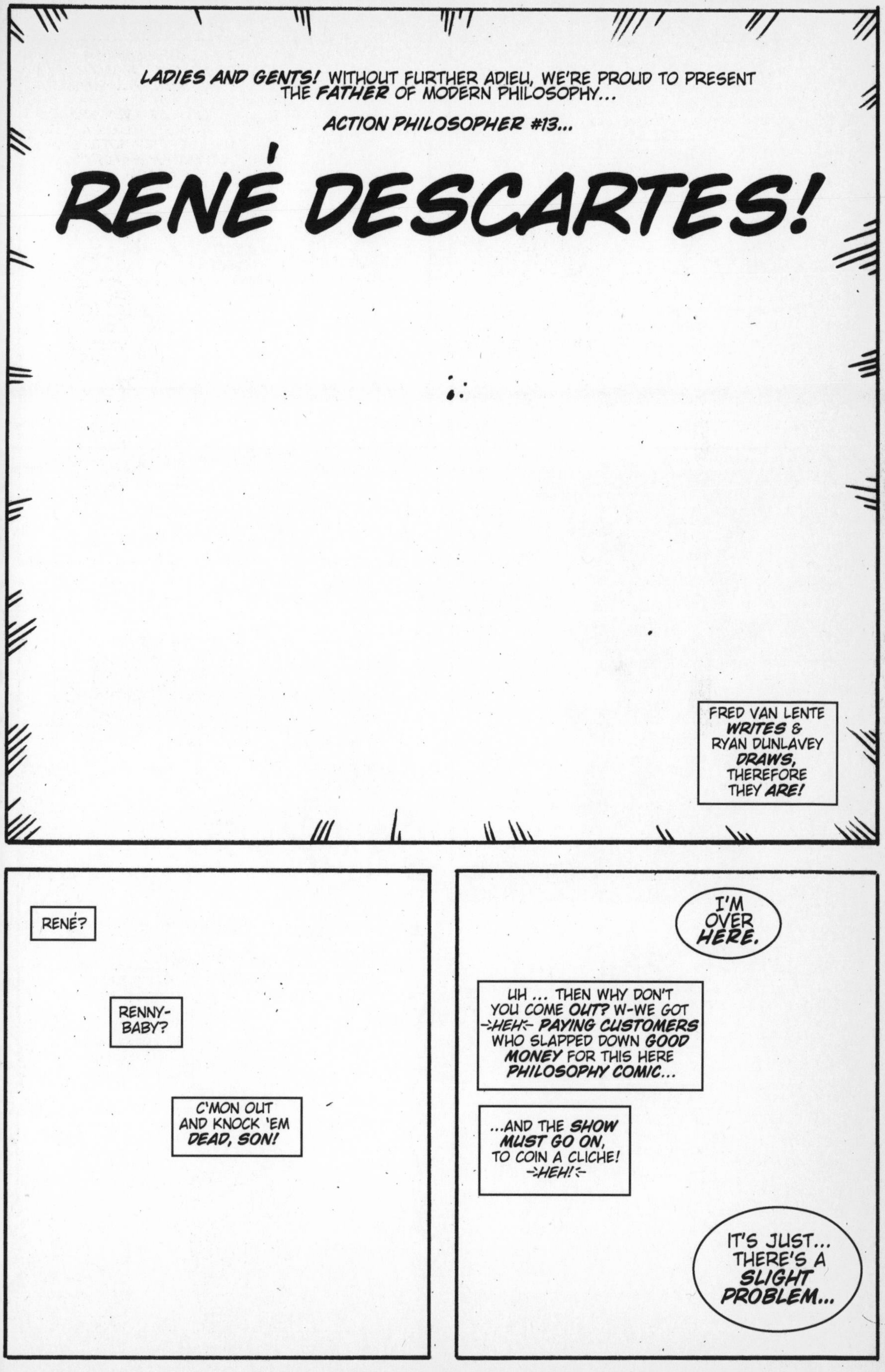

LADIES AND GENTS! WITHOUT FURTHER ADIEU, WE'RE PROUD TO PRESENT THE *FATHER* OF MODERN PHILOSOPHY...

ACTION PHILOSOPHER #13...

RENÉ DESCARTES!

FRED VAN LENTE *WRITES* & RYAN DUNLAVEY *DRAWS*, THEREFORE THEY *ARE!*

RENÉ?

RENNY-BABY?

C'MON OUT AND KNOCK 'EM *DEAD, SON!*

I'M OVER *HERE.*

UH ... THEN WHY DON'T YOU COME *OUT?* W-WE GOT *-HEH-* *PAYING CUSTOMERS* WHO SLAPPED DOWN *GOOD MONEY* FOR THIS HERE *PHILOSOPHY COMIC...*

...AND THE *SHOW MUST GO ON,* TO COIN A CLICHE! *-HEH!-*

IT'S JUST... THERE'S A *SLIGHT PROBLEM...*

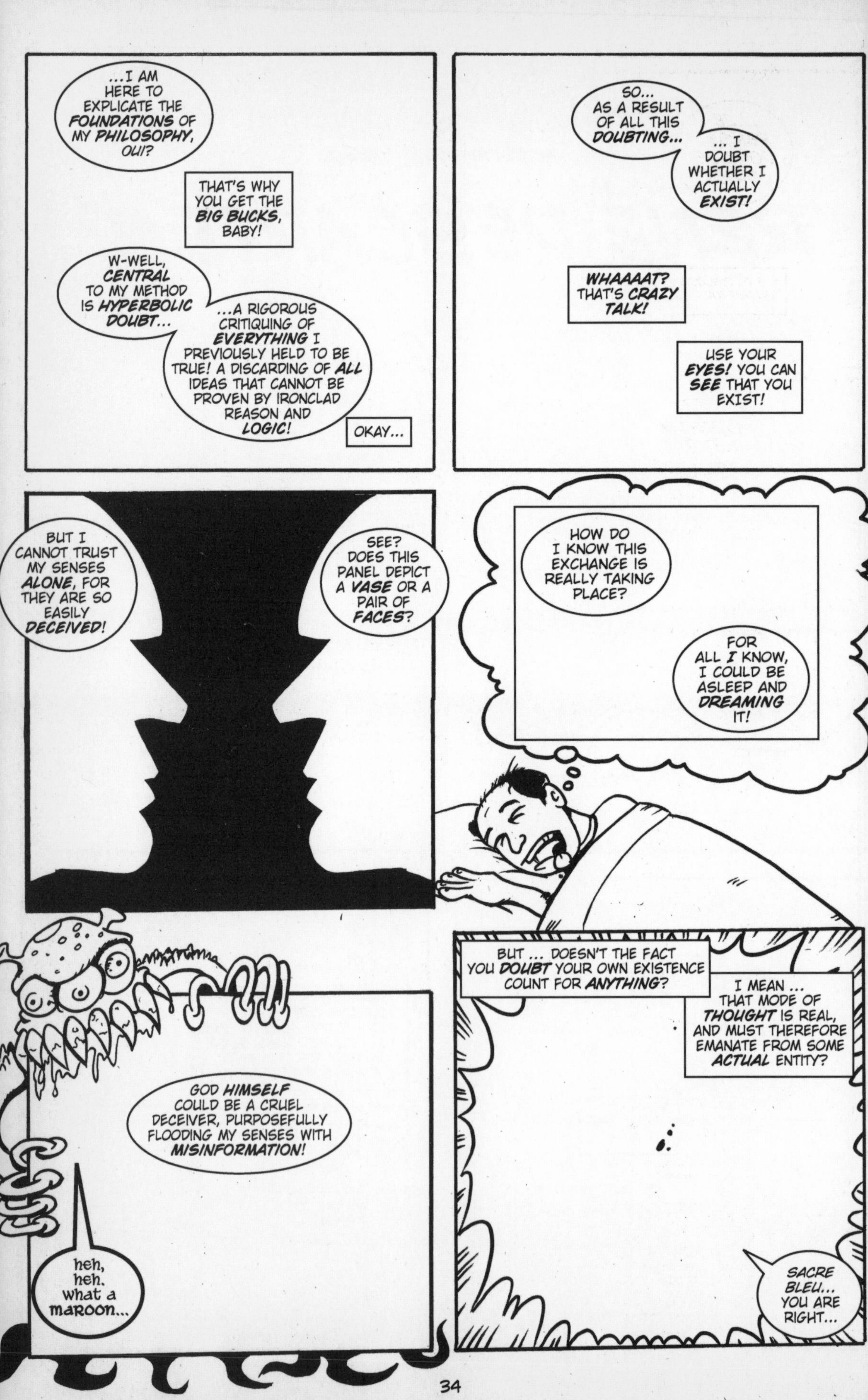
...I AM HERE TO EXPLICATE THE FOUNDATIONS OF MY PHILOSOPHY, OUI?
THAT'S WHY YOU GET THE BIG BUCKS, BABY!
W-WELL, CENTRAL TO MY METHOD IS HYPERBOLIC DOUBT...
...A RIGOROUS CRITIQUING OF EVERYTHING I PREVIOUSLY HELD TO BE TRUE! A DISCARDING OF ALL IDEAS THAT CANNOT BE PROVEN BY IRONCLAD REASON AND LOGIC!
OKAY...
SO... AS A RESULT OF ALL THIS DOUBTING...
... I DOUBT WHETHER I ACTUALLY EXIST!
WHAAAAT? THAT'S CRAZY TALK!
USE YOUR EYES! YOU CAN SEE THAT YOU EXIST!
BUT I CANNOT TRUST MY SENSES ALONE, FOR THEY ARE SO EASILY DECEIVED!
SEE? DOES THIS PANEL DEPICT A VASE OR A PAIR OF FACES?
HOW DO I KNOW THIS EXCHANGE IS REALLY TAKING PLACE?
FOR ALL I KNOW, I COULD BE ASLEEP AND DREAMING IT!
GOD HIMSELF COULD BE A CRUEL DECEIVER, PURPOSEFULLY FLOODING MY SENSES WITH MISINFORMATION!
heh, heh. what a maroon...
BUT ... DOESN'T THE FACT YOU DOUBT YOUR OWN EXISTENCE COUNT FOR ANYTHING?
I MEAN ... THAT MODE OF THOUGHT IS REAL, AND MUST THEREFORE EMANATE FROM SOME ACTUAL ENTITY?
SACRE BLEU... YOU ARE RIGHT...

...JE PENSE, DONC JE SUIS!*
I THINK, THEREFORE I AM!***
*: R.D., DISCOURSE ON METHOD (1637)
COGITO, ERGO SUM!**
***: THIS COMIC. JUST NOW.
**: R.D., MEDIATIONS ON FIRST PHILOSOPHY (1641)
MY SOUL HOLDS THIS IDEA WITH SUCH CLEAR AND DISTINCT CERTAINTY THAT IT MUST BE TRUE.
SUCH CLARITY SHALL MAKE AN EXCELLENT CRITERION AS I REVIEW THE OTHER IDEAS IN MY MIND TO SEE WHETHER OR NOT THEY ARE TRUE AS WELL.
MY SENSES SUGGEST THAT MY SOUL/MIND IS ATTACHED TO SOME KIND OF BODY!
EXTENDED SUBSTANCE -- RES EXTENSA -- FROM MY RES COGITANS -- THINKING SUBSTANCE!
BUT... MY SENSES ARE UNTRUSTWORTHY INFORMANTS!
WHEN I LOOK ACROSS THE STREET AND SEE PEOPLE WALKING THERE, ALL I REALLY KNOW ARE MOVING CLOTHES!
HOW DO I KNOW THAT THOSE ARE REALLY PEOPLE WALKING AND NOT JUST TEXTILE-WRAPPED AUTOMATONS?
BECAUSE MY MIND HAS AJUDGED THAT THEY ARE!
AWARENESS OF THE CONTENTS OF THE MIND PRECEDES ANY AWARENESS OF EXTERNAL REALITY!

AN INVENTORY OF MY MIND'S **CONTENTS** REVEALS THREE DISTINCT **TYPES** OF IDEAS:

FICTITIOUS IDEAS, WHICH THE MIND ***INVENTS...***

...ADVENTITIOUS IDEAS, WHICH THE MIND ***RECEIVES*** FROM THE ***EXTERNAL WORLD...***

....AND ***INATE*** IDEAS, WHICH ARE BORN ***WITH*** THE MIND!

IRONICALLY, THE ONLY CATEGORY I CAN BE ***SURE*** EXISTS IS ***FICTION,*** SINCE IT PRESUPPOSES THE EXISTENCE OF MY ***MIND*** (WHICH IS ***ALL*** I HAVE PROVEN EXISTS)!

NOR CAN A CAUSE CREATE AN EFFECT THAT IS MORE PERFECT THAN ITSELF!
(EVEN THOUGH I CAN IMAGINE THE FICTITIOUS IDEA OF THE "PERFECT WOMAN," I CANNOT ACTUALIZE THE PERFECT WOMAN MYSELF!)
SIGH... BACK TO THE DRAWING BOARD...
IT FOLLOWS, THEN, THAT FALLIBLE, FINITE ME COULD ONLY HAVE BEEN CAUSED BY A PERFECT, INFINITE SOURCE!
IN OTHER WORDS, I EXIST--
--THEREFORE, GOD EXISTS!
(THOUGH IT IS THEORETICALLY POSSIBLE I COULD HAVE BEEN CREATED BY A CAUSE EQUAL TO ME...
...THAT FINITE, FALLIBLE CAUSE WOULD HAVE THE IDEA OF THE INFINITE PERFECT AS WELL, WHICH MUST HAVE BEEN IMPLANTED BY AN INFINITELY PERFECT SOURCE!)
APROVED BY INSPECTOR
OUR INNATE IDEA OF THE INFINITELY PERFECT GOD IS THE MARK OF THE CRAFTSMAN STAMPED ON HIS WORK!
IF GOD IS PERFECT, IT FOLLOWS THAT HE IS NOT A DECEIVER!
ONE DISSEMBLES ONLY TO PROTECT VULNERABILITIES, WHICH A PERFECT BEING WOULD NOT HAVE!
AND SINCE GOD CREATED MY SENSES, MEMORY, AND OTHER INTELLECTUAL FACULTIES, AND SINCE HE IS NOT A DECEIVER...
...THEN MY SENSES, ON THE WHOLE, CAN BE TRUSTED!

YET THIS ALLEGED "EXTERNAL WORLD" (WHICH I HAVE NOT YET PROVEN EXISTS) EVIDENCES TWO VERY DIFFERENT SETS OF PROPERTIES!
MY EYES TELL ME THE SUN IS VERY SMALL, AND THE SENSATION OF HEAT ON MY SKIN SUGGESTS IT IS VERY CLOSE BY!

BUT MY MIND KNOWS THAT THIS IS NOT TRUE! ASTRONOMICAL AND MATHEMATICAL DATA SHOW THAT THE SUN IS BOTH VERY BIG AND VERY FAR AWAY!
THESE INHERENT FACTORS OF THE SUN'S BEING--VOLUME AND DISTANCE--ARE ITS PRIMARY PROPERTIES! AND DERIVING FROM THOSE ARE SECONDARY PROPERTIES SUCH AS COLOR AND ODOR!

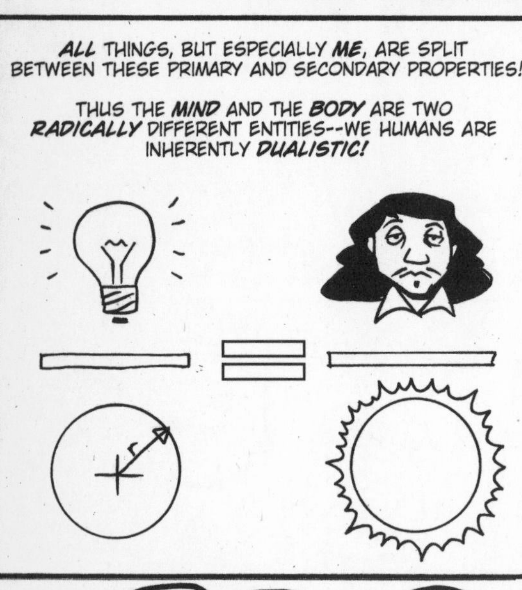
ALL THINGS, BUT ESPECIALLY ME, ARE SPLIT BETWEEN THESE PRIMARY AND SECONDARY PROPERTIES!
THUS THE MIND AND THE BODY ARE TWO RADICALLY DIFFERENT ENTITIES--WE HUMANS ARE INHERENTLY DUALISTIC!
r

SINCE MY SENSES ARE PART OF MY BODY AND NOT OF MY MIND, I CANNOT BE CREATING THESE STIMULI MYSELF (I.E., THROUGH INVENTED IDEAS).
GOD COULD NOT BE FEEDING THESE SECONDARY PROPERTIES DIRECTLY TO ME, SINCE WE HAVE ESTABLISHED THAT HE IS NOT A DECEIVER.
HOKUM

NOR COULD I BE DREAMING THESE SECONDARY PROPERTIES, FOR MEMORY TIES THE EVENTS OF OUR WAKING LIVES TOGETHER.
(IN A DREAM I DO NOT REMEMBER ALL THE DREAMS I HAD BEFORE THAT ONE.)
I REMEMBER ALL OF MY LIFE UP UNTIL THIS POINT, SO I MUST BE AWAKE!

THEREFORE... I HAVE NO OTHER CHOICE BUT TO CONCLUDE...
...THAT I RECEIVE PASSIVE PERCEPTIONS OF AN EXTERNAL WORLD...

DESCARTES HIT UPON HIS REVOLUTIONARY METHODOLOGY WHILE SERVING IN THE THIRTY YEARS WAR.
IN NOVEMBER 1619 HE FOUND HIMSELF STUCK IN A SNOWBOUND LITTLE ROOM IN NEUBERG, GERMANY.
...BECAUSE AN EXTERNAL WORLD ACTUALLY EXISTS!

LITTLE WONDER HIS MIND SOON TURNED TOWARD PHILOSOPHICAL PURSUITS.
SOOOOO BOOOOORRRED...
HEY...I WONDER IF IT'D EVER BE POSSIBLE FOR ALL HUMAN KNOWLEDGE TO ATTAIN THE PRECISE ACCURACY OF MATHEMATICS?

THAT EVENING, THE YOUNG SOLDIER HAD A DREAM THAT CONVINCED HIM THAT GOD HAD INDEED SHOWN HIM THE CLEAREST PATH TO TRUTH.
AS LONG AS THE MIND IS CAREFUL TO AVOID THE PITFALLS LAID OUT FOR IT BY THE BODY'S FAULTY PERCEPTIONS...
...ABSOLUTE KNOWLEDGE OF ALL THINGS IS ATTAINABLE BY HUMAN REASON!

DESCARTES APPLIED HIS EXACTING METHOD TO PHYSICS, ASTRONOMY, PSYCHOLOGY, ANATOMY, AND, MOST FAMOUSLY, MATH.
NATURE CAN BE DEFINED THROUGH NUMBERS!
HIS SYSTEM OF CARTESIAN COORDINATES FORMED THE BEDROCK OF ANALYTICAL GEOMETRY!
Z
Y
X
RENÉ

HE ALSO WROTE A COMPREHENSIVE TREATISE ON PHYSICS, THE WORLD, BUT CHANGED HIS MIND ABOUT PUBLISHING IT ONCE GALILEO WAS PUT ON TRIAL FOR SUPPORTING SIMILAR IDEAS.
YOU GOT A PROBLEM WITH THAT, FRENCHIE?
WHO, ME? >HEH!<... NON!
"THE WORLD"

UNFORTUNATELY FOR HIM, HIS FAME REACHED THE ECCENTRIC YOUNG QUEEN OF SWEDEN, CHRISTINA.
I HAVE THE BEST OF EVERYTHING...
...I WANT THE BEST PHILOSOPHY TUTOR TOO! BRING THE FRENCHMAN TO ME!
Y-YES, MUM!

CHRISTINA SCHEDULED THEIR SESSIONS FOR 5AM SHARP, THREE DAYS A WEEK.
A-CHOO! !@#$! SWEDISH WINTERS!!
TWO MONTHS INTO HIS NEW JOB, DESCARTES CAUGHT A COLD THAT QUICKLY SNOWBALLED INTO PNEUMONIA.

HE STRUGGLED FOR A WEEK, THEN DIED ON FEB. 11, 1650...
SPARE THE FRENCH BLOOD! >GAK!<
...AT 4AM, PERHAPS TO AVOID ANOTHER APPOINTMENT WITH THE KOOKY QUEEN!

MANY BELIEVED THAT SINCE DESCARTES HAD LOGICALLY PROVEN GOD'S EXISTENCE, HE WOULD BE A SHOO-IN FOR SAINTHOOD!
AS HIS BODY WAS TRANSPORTED BACK TO FRANCE, OVER-EAGER PILGRIMS PICKED APART THE CORPSE FOR RELICS!
FRANCE
LOOK, MA! I GOT THE DRUMSTICK! AYUK!

ONE OF THE MOST REVERED FIGURES IN FRENCH HISTORY, DESCARTES WAS LAID TO REST AT THE CATHEDRAL OF ST. GERMAIN DES PRES IN PARIS'S LATIN QUARTER...

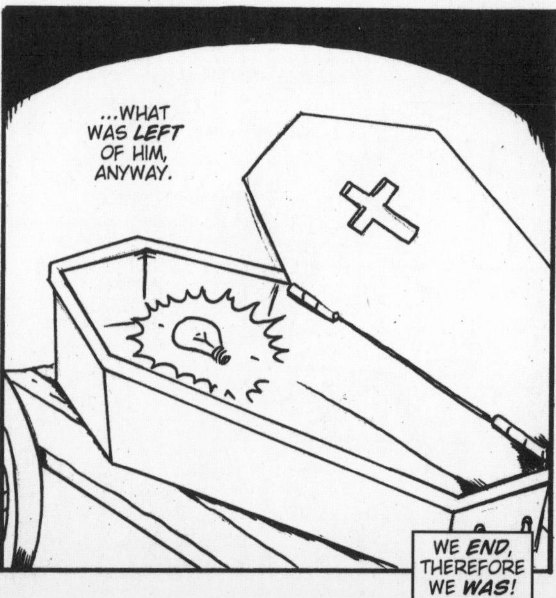
...WHAT WAS LEFT OF HIM, ANYWAY.
WE END, THEREFORE WE WAS!

WHEN YOU THINK OF A *"PHILOSOPHER"*, ODDS ARE YOU THINK OF A BRAINY, TWEEDY GUY WRITING IN A CAFE, SUCKING DOWN COFFEE AND CIGARETTES, ENGAGING IN HEATED *METAPHYSICAL DEBATES* WITH HIS *INTELLECTUAL BUDDIES...*

...WHEN *REALLY*, WHAT YOU'RE THINKING OF IS *ACTION PHILOSOPHER #14:*

JEAN-PAUL SARTRE

HELL IS *FRED VAN LENTE* (WRITER) & *RYAN DUNLAVEY* (ARTIST)!

THE *TIME*? AUGUST 1940!

THE *PLACE? STALAG 12D*, A PRISONER-OF-WAR CAMP OUTSIDE *TRIER*, GERMANY!

LOOK, KAROL! THE GOOSE-STEPPERS BROUGHT US SOME *FRENCH CHICKENS* FOR DINNER! >BWOK, BWOK!<

HEY JAN, HOW MANY *FRENCH TROOPS* DOES IT TAKE TO DEFEND *PARIS*?

HOW MANY?

WHO KNOWS? THEY'VE NEVER TRIED!
!@$%! POLES!!
HAHAHA!!
AMONG THE NEW P.O.W.'S IS THE 35 YEAR-OLD SARTRE...

...LATELY OF THE METEREOLOGICAL CORPS.
THURSDAY'S FORECAST CALLS FOR A HEAVY NAZI FRONT TO MOVE IN FROM THE EAST...
FRANCE
...FOLLOWED BY PERIODS OF SCATTERED COLLABORATION UNTIL 1944!
UP NEXT: PIERRE WITH SPORTS!

THOUGH STALAG 12D'S POLISH AND CZECH PRISONERS MOCKED THE FRENCH AS COWARDS, REALLY THEY WERE UNDONE BY GOVERNMENTAL INCOMPETENCE.
AW-HAW-HAW! I WOULD LOVE TO SEE ZEE KRAUTS GET PAST OUR IMPREGNABLE MAGINOT LINE!
UH... SIR...
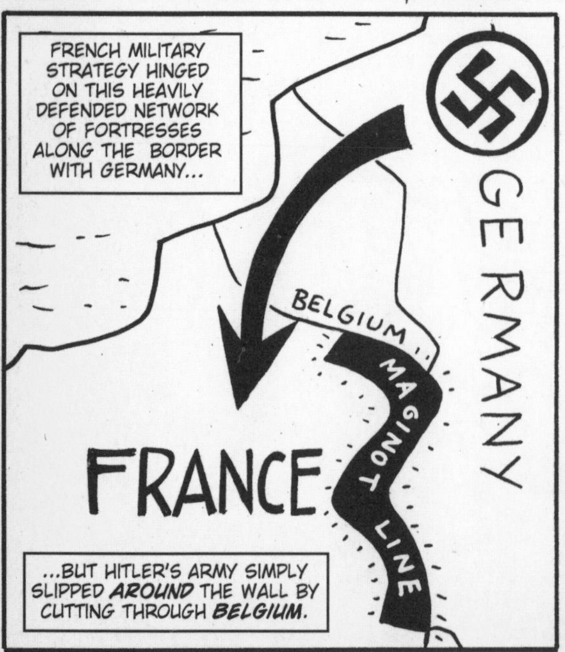
FRENCH MILITARY STRATEGY HINGED ON THIS HEAVILY DEFENDED NETWORK OF FORTRESSES ALONG THE BORDER WITH GERMANY...
GERMANY
BELGIUM
MAGINOT LINE
FRANCE
...BUT HITLER'S ARMY SIMPLY SLIPPED AROUND THE WALL BY CUTTING THROUGH BELGIUM.

SARTRE'S UNIT WAS CAPTURED ON JUNE 21--HIS BIRTHDAY--AND HE IMMEDIATELY BECAME STALAG 12D'S BIGGEST CELEBRITY, ALREADY FAMOUS AS THE AUTHOR OF SUCH NOVELS AS NAUSEA (1938).
A PHILOSOPHY TEACHER BY PROFESSION, HE BEGAN GIVING AVIDLY-ATTENDED LECTURES ON THE SUBJECT EVERY TUESDAY.

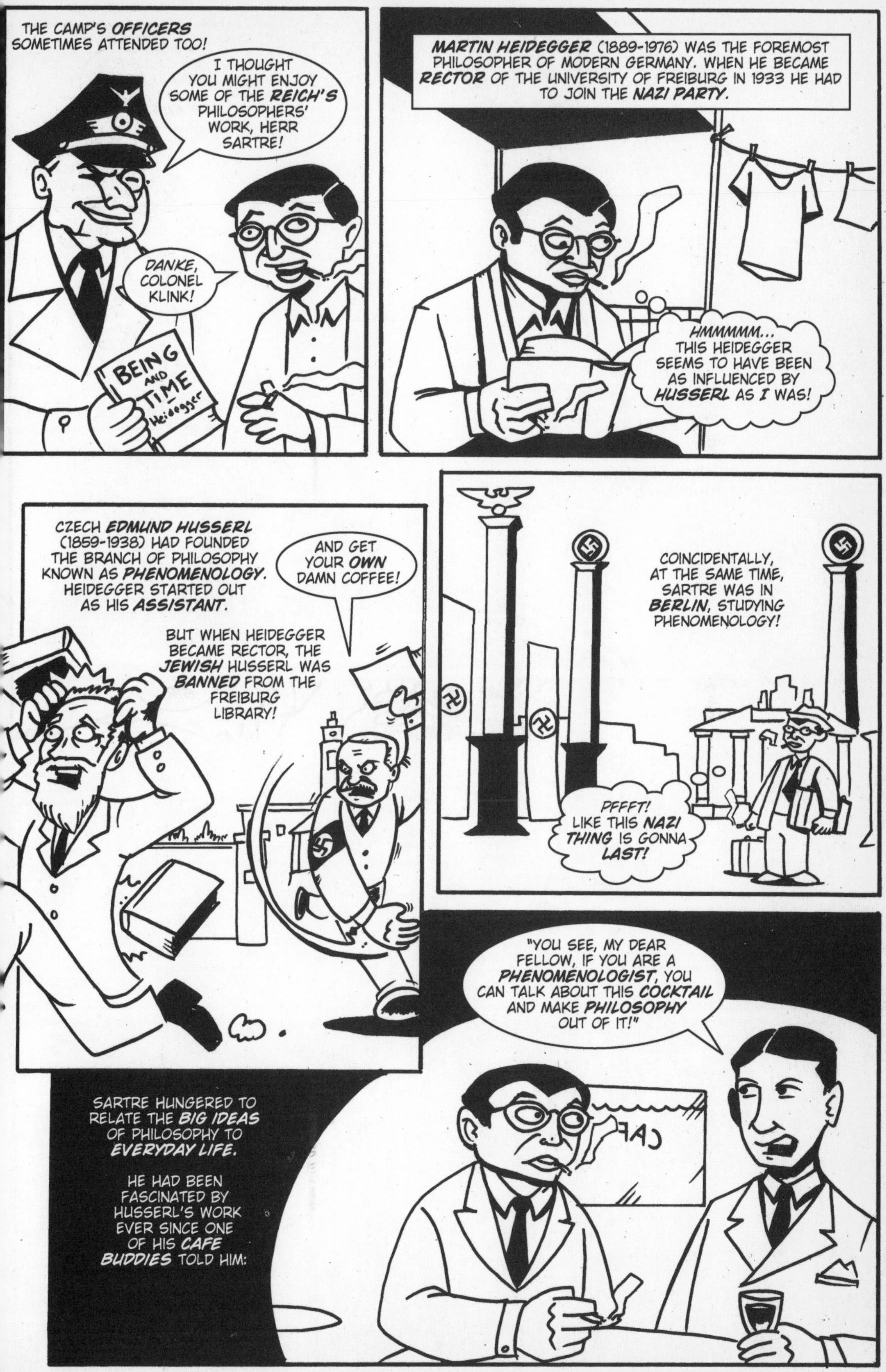

CZECH **EDMUND HUSSERL** (1859-1938) HAD FOUNDED THE BRANCH OF PHILOSOPHY KNOWN AS **PHENOMENOLOGY**. HEIDEGGER STARTED OUT AS HIS **ASSISTANT**.

AND GET YOUR **OWN** DAMN COFFEE!

BUT WHEN HEIDEGGER BECAME RECTOR, THE **JEWISH** HUSSERL WAS **BANNED** FROM THE FREIBURG LIBRARY!

COINCIDENTALLY, AT THE SAME TIME, SARTRE WAS IN **BERLIN**, STUDYING PHENOMENOLOGY!

PFFFT! LIKE THIS **NAZI THING** IS GONNA **LAST!**

SARTRE HUNGERED TO RELATE THE ***BIG IDEAS*** OF PHILOSOPHY TO ***EVERYDAY LIFE***.

HE HAD BEEN FASCINATED BY HUSSERL'S WORK EVER SINCE ONE OF HIS ***CAFE BUDDIES*** TOLD HIM:

"YOU SEE, MY DEAR FELLOW, IF YOU ARE A **PHENOMENOLOGIST**, YOU CAN TALK ABOUT THIS **COCKTAIL** AND MAKE **PHILOSOPHY** OUT OF IT!"

HUSSERL WROTE THAT, "PHENOMENOLOGY MUST HONOR DESCARTES AS ITS GENUINE PATRIARCH," BUT HE FELT...
DESCARTES WASN'T EXTREME ENOUGH!
WICKED AWESOME DUDE!!

HUSSERL TOOK ISSUE WITH THE "I THINK" PART OF "I THINK, THEREFORE I AM."
AFTER ALL, NO ONE JUST "THINKS!"
REALLY? NOT EVEN ME?
NOT EVEN YOU, BIG GUY!

ONE ALWAYS THINKS ABOUT SOMETHING!
THERE IS ALWAYS AN OBJECT OF CONSCIOUSNESS!

FOR THIS REASON HUSSERL WHOLLY REJECTED THE CARTESIAN NOTION THAT ONE COULD APPLY PSEUDO-SCIENTIFIC "OBJECTIVE" LOGIC TO CONSCIOUSNESS!
PHILOSOPHY LAB
SHOO! BAD SCIENTISTS! SHOO!

THE ONLY ACCURATE WAY TO EVALUATE CONSCIOUSNESS IS THROUGH "PURE SUBJECTIVITY" -- THE INTERNAL MONOLOGUE THAT APPREHENDS REALITY AS A SERIES OF EXPERIENCED OBJECTS...
THE INTERSECTION OF SUNSET & VINE WAS SLICK WITH THE TEARS OF FALLEN ANGELS...
SMOKE
BAR
... A/K/A PHENOMENA!

HUSSERL ALSO SAID THAT CONSCIOUSNESS IS FUNDAMENTALLY *INTENTIONAL*. SARTRE WOULD LATER ILLUSTRATE THIS POINT THUSLY:
"I HAVE AN APPOINTMENT WITH PETER AT 4 O'CLOCK. I ARRIVE AT THE CAFE A QUARTER OF AN HOUR *LATE*."
"PETER IS *ALWAYS* PUNCTUAL. WILL HE HAVE *WAITED* FOR ME?"

"WHEN I ENTER THIS CAFE TO SEARCH FOR PETER, THERE IS FORMED A *SYNTHETIC ORGANIZATION* OF ALL THE OBJECTS IN THE CAFE, AS THE GROUND ON WHICH PETER IS GIVEN AS *ABOUT* TO APPEAR."
"I AM WITNESS TO THE SUCCESSIVE DISAPPEARANCE OF ALL THE OBJECTS WHICH I LOOK AT--IN PARTICULAR OF THE *FACES*, WHICH DETAIN ME FOR AN INSTANT (COULD *THIS* BE PETER)?"

SO A CAFE IS NEVER "OBJECTIVELY" *JUST* A CAFE! IN *THIS* INSTANCE, IT HAS BEEN *CONSTRUCTED* BY SARTRE'S CONSCIOUSNESS AS *"THE SPACE WHERE PETER COULD BE"*!
?

DESCARTES' *ERROR* WAS TO THINK OF CONSCIOUSNESS AS SOMEHOW *TRANSCENDENT* FROM REALITY, LOOKING *DOWN* ON IT!
NO
YES
BUT REALLY, YOU EXIST *WITHIN* THE WORLD, AND IT IS ONLY *THROUGH* YOUR CONSCIOUSNESS THAT YOU CAN MAKE *ANY* SENSE OF THE WORLD AT ALL!

STILL NOT *CONVINCED*? TAKE THE EXAMPLE OF A *CUBE*.
EVERY *SCHOOLCHILD* KNOWS THAT A CUBE, TO *BE* A CUBE, *MUST* HAVE *SIX SIDES*.
BUT *WHY*? YOU'VE NEVER *SEEN* A CUBE WITH SIX SIDES. YOU CAN ONLY SEE (OR *DRAW*) *THREE* SIDES AT A TIME!
ONE... TWO... *CRAP!!*

FOR A CUBE TO EXIST AS A PROPER WHOLE IN YOUR MIND, YOUR ABSTRACT IMAGINATION *MUST* CONSTRUCT IT!
I CALL IT *"CUBIST CUBE!"*
YOU *SHOULD* HAVE JUST CALLED IT *"SUCK."*

HEIDEGGER, HOWEVER, THOUGHT THAT HUSSERL DIDN'T GO FAR ENOUGH!
DUUUUUUUDE!!!

HIS MAJOR OBJECTION TO TRADITIONAL PHILOSOPHY WAS THAT IT TREATED THE BEING OF MAN IN THE SAME WAY AS THE BEING OF THINGS.
WHY DO I EXIST?
THINGS DON'T DO THAT -- ONLY THE BEING OF MAN INCLUDES AWARENESS OF HIS BEING!
IN BEING AND TIME, HEIDEGGER INSISTS THAT HUMAN BEINGS SHOULD BE DESCRIBED NOT AS OBJECTS, BUT AS "DASEIN"--
LIFE IS A STATE OF MIND.
--OR IN ENGLISH, "BEING THERE!"
"THE WORLD IS NOT A WAY OF CHARACTERIZING THOSE ENTITIES DASEIN IS NOT," HEIDEGGER WRITES.
"IT IS RATHER A CHARACTERISTIC OF DASEIN ITSELF!"

FOR EXAMPLE, TAKE A HAMMER, WHICH WE FIRST ENCOUNTER AS A UTENSIL WITH WHICH WE CAN ACCOMPLISH SOME TASK.

THE MORE WE HAMMER, THE LESS WE NOTICE THE HAMMER AS DISTINCT FROM OURSELVES.
NOR CAN WE SEPARATE THE HAMMER ITSELF FROM HOW IT FITS INTO THE TASK AT HAND!

THIS IS WHAT HEIDEGGER MEANS WHEN HE SAYS THAT DASEIN IS THE WORLD:
WE PROJECT OUR NETWORK OF PURPOSES ONTO ITEMS IN THE WORLD AND THUS MAKE THEM WHAT THEY ARE!

WHEN DASEIN CONTEMPLATES HIS OWN EXISTENCE, HE CANNOT HELP BUT PROJECT ONTO IT TIME---
SARTRE
APRIL
--I.E., MORTALITY-- THE REALIZATION HE WILL ONE DAY END!

WE DO NOT "FEAR" DEATH -- FEAR IS A RESPONSE TO AN OBJECT, A TEMPORAL THREAT AGAINST WHICH WE CAN FIGHT OR FLEE!

DEATH, AFTER ALL, IS INEVITABLE AND INDEFENSIBLE.
NO, HEIDEGGER SAYS, WHAT WE FEEL TOWARDS DEATH IS ANXIETY--FOR, UNLIKE FEAR, ANXIETY HAS NO OBJECT! IT IS A CONSTANT NAGGING DREAD OF, LITERALLY, "NO-THING"!

HMMM... ANOTHER WAY OF FORMULATING THE DILEMMA IS: DASEIN IS ANXIOUS BECAUSE HE IS CONSCIOUS OF BEING HIS OWN FUTURE!
"CONSCIOUSNESS IS A BEING, THE NATURE OF WHICH IS TO BE CONSCIOUS OF THE NOTHINGNESS OF ITS BEING!"

IN THE FACE OF DEATH, ONLY MAN CAN MAKE HIMSELF!
ONLY HE, USING HIS INTENTIONAL CONSCIOUSNESS, CAN CHOOSE ACTS THAT LEAD HIM TO HIS IDEAL SELF!

THAT MEANS--
--MANKIND IS CONDEMNED TO BE FREE!
UH... YOU BLIND, MAN?

SARTRE RADICALLY REVERSED MILLENNIA OF PHILOSOPHICAL THOUGHT, WHICH, EVER SINCE PLATO, HAD HELD...
EXISTENCE EMANATES FROM A HIGHER ESSENCE!

NON! EXISTENCE PRECEDES ESSENCE!
DASEIN AND ONLY DASEIN IMPOSES VALUE ON BEINGS-IN-THEMSELVES!
NOOOOOO !!!!!

"WHILE DASEIN IS LE POUR-SOI -- BEING-FOR-ITSELF!
YOU ARE YOUR OWN OBJECT OF CONSCIOUSNESS!"
WITH GREAT EXISTENCE COMES GREAT RESPONSIBILITY!
BAT PANTS
SEX MEN
HARRY FISH
WOLVER GROIN
GIANT SIZE BIG PENIS
SKANK QUILITY
THE SHUT-UPS
TURDS OF PREY
SANDWICH
54 1/2
AAAAAAAHH!!

THE AWESOMENESS OF THIS RESPONSIBILITY IS TERRIFYING TO THE INDIVIDUAL! THIS IS WHY SARTRE SAYS WE ARE CONDEMNED TO BE FREE:
WAAAA! LEMME IN!
NEIN!
"ONE SENSES ONE'S TRUE RELATION TO ONESELF AND TO OTHERS, BECAUSE ONE FLEES IT."

"WE ARE ALWAYS READY TO TAKE REFUGE IN A BELIEF IN DETERMINISM IF THIS FREEDOM WEIGHS UPON US OR WE NEED AN EXCUSE."
STUFF WILL HAPPEN TO YOU!
STUFF?!? TO ME?!? REALLY?!?
"WE FLEE FROM ANXIETY BY ATTEMPTING TO APPREHEND OURSELVES FROM WITHOUT AS AN OTHER OR AS A THING."

THE MYTH OF GOD, FOR INSTANCE, WAS A WAY OF LITERALLY BECOMING THE OBJECT OF A HIGHER CONSCIOUSNESS! BUT...
WAAAA! DON'T GO!
SEE YA IN THE FUNNY PAGES, KID!
Science Sez: YER FIRED!

SARTRE STARTED TEACHING HEIDEGGER, MIXED WITH HIS OWN THEORIES, THREE TIMES A WEEK!
EACH MAN IS NOTHING MORE AND NOTHING LESS THAN THE SUM OF HIS ACTIONS!

UNTIL THE SPRING OF 1941...
UGH! WE HAVE TOO MANY FRENCH PRISONERS!
MAYBE WE COULD PARDON THE CIVILIANS?

USING PHONY DOCUMENTS THAT SAID HE WAS CIVILIAN -- AS WELL AS PLAYING UP A NEAR-BLIND RIGHT EYE THAT HE SAID WOULD RENDER HIM USELESS TO THE MILITARY...
HEY...YOU THINK THIS WOULD MAKE A GOOD WACKY AMERICAN SIT-COM, A BUNCH OF P.O.W.'S CONSTANTLY TRYING TO ESCAPE FROM A GERMAN CAMP?
ARE YOU HIGH?

...SARTRE AND A PRIEST BUDDY WON THEIR EARLY RELEASE!
SARRRRTRE!
SNAP!
HE RETURNED TO OCCUPIED PARIS, WHERE HE CONTINUED WORKING ON THE MONUMENTAL TREATISE HE BEGAN IN STALAG 12D: BEING AND NOTHINGNESS.
-SIGH!- WE'VE NEVER BEEN MORE FREE!
UH... YOU BLIND, MAN?

"WE HAD LOST ALL OUR RIGHTS," SARTRE WROTE AFTER LIBERATION, "AND BECAUSE OF ALL THIS WE WERE FREE."
"EXILE, CAPTIVITY, AND ESPECIALLY DEATH (WHICH WE USUALLY SHRINK FROM FACING AT ALL IN HAPPIER DAYS) BECAME FOR US THE HABITUAL OBJECTS OF OUR CONCERN."

"AND THE CHOICE THAT EACH OF US MADE OF HIS LIFE WAS AN AUTHENTIC CHOICE BECAUSE IT WAS MADE FACE TO FACE WITH DEATH, BECAUSE IT COULD ALWAYS HAVE BEEN EXPRESSED IN THESE TERMS:"
'RATHER DEATH THAN...'

"HERE I AM NOT SPEAKING OF THE ELITE AMONG US WHO WERE REAL RESISTANTS, BUT OF ALL FRENCHMEN WHO, AT EVERY HOUR OF THE NIGHT AND DAY THROUGHOUT FOUR YEARS, ANSWERED:"
NO!

THOUGH IT'S FREQUENTLY ASSERTED THAT SARTRE WAS A MEMBER OF THE ***ARMED*** FRENCH RESISTANCE, THAT'S NOT TRUE.

HIS OWN "NO" TOOK EFFECT ON THE ***STAGE.*** HE HAD WRITTEN A ***CHRISTMAS PAGEANT*** FOR STALAG 12D AND DISCOVERED HE ENJOYED ***PLAYWRITING***.

ORESTES SOON REALIZES THAT THE FURIES HAVE NO POWER OVER HIM ONCE HE ACCEPTS HIS ACTS AS HIS OWN!
"I AM MY FREEDOM! NO SOONER HAD ZEUS CREATED ME THAN I CEASED TO BE HIS!"
EXIT
CURSES! FOILED AGAIN!

HE LIBERATES THE PEOPLE OF ARGOS (FRENCH COLLABORATORS?) FROM ZEUS'S TYRANNY...
THANKS A LOT, JERK!
INGRATES.
...AND THEY HATE HIM FOR IT!

THE PEOPLE OF ARGOS EXEMPLIFY MAN'S MOST COMMON RETREAT FROM HIS TERRIFYING FREEDOM...INTO WHAT WE WOULD TODAY LIKELY TERM DENIAL...
IT'S NOT JUST A RIVER IN EGYPT!
...BUT SARTRE PREFERRED TO CALL MAUVAISE FOI... "BAD FAITH"!
HE WOULD EXPLORE THIS CONCEPT MOST FULLY IN HIS NEXT PLAY, NO EXIT (1944).

THE ACTION TAKES PLACE IN EXISTENTIALIST HELL.
YOU KNOW... THIS DOESN'T SEEM SO BAD.
EACH OF THE CHARACTERS HAS BEEN DAMNED FOR LEADING INAUTHENTIC LIVES.
TRUTH BY GARCIN
GARCIN, FOR EXAMPLE, IS A REPORTER WHO FANCIES HIMSELF HEROIC.

BUT WHEN WAR DOES BREAK OUT, HE TRIES TO FLEE THE COUNTRY, AND IS CAPTURED AND SHOT AS A COWARD AND A DESERTER!
WELCOME TO MEXICO

IN HELL, HE IS CONDEMNED TO SPEND ETERNITY WITH TWO PEOPLE WHO REFUSE TO ENABLE HIS NARCISSISTIC DENIAL! HE'LL FOREVER BE REMINDED HE NEVER EVEN TRIED TO ACTUALIZE HIS HEROIC IDEALS!
TRUTH BY GARCIN
≠

HENCE THE DRAMA'S MOST FAMOUS LINE:
HELL IS OTHER PEOPLE!

THE ALLIES FINALLY LIBERATED PARIS IN 1944!
THOUGH BEING AND NOTHINGNESS HAD BEEN PUBLISHED THE YEAR BEFORE, WITH THE WAR OVER IT COULD NOW REACH A WIDE AUDIENCE.

SARTRE SUCCEEDED IN MAKING PHILOSOPHY INTELLIGIBLE TO THE REGULAR PERSON! HE BECAME HUGELY FAMOUS-- AND HIS PHILOSOPHY, KNOWN AS "EXISTENTIALISM", BECAME A POPULAR BUZZWORD!
CAFE
UNFORTUNATELY, THIS HAD SOME NEGATIVE SIDE-EFFECTS...
...LIKE HE COULD NO LONGER GET WORK DONE IN CAFES!

SARTRE'S EXPERIENCE WITH ***COLLECTIVE LIVING*** IN STALAG 12D LED HIS POLITICS TO DRIFT ***LEFTWARD***, TOWARD ***SOCIALISM***.
UH...NOT SURE WHERE MY ***MATERIALISTIC DETERMINISM*** FITS INTO THIS WHOLE "MAN IS CONDEMNED TO BE ***FREE***" BUSINESS...
YADDA, YADDA, YADDA...

HE TOOK HIS STRONGEST ACTIVIST STANDS AGAINST ***COLONIALISM*** IN ALL ITS FORMS--ATTACKING THE U.S. FOR BOMBING ***VIETNAM*** AND THE U.S.S.R. FOR CRUSHING THE ***HUNGARIAN*** UPRISING!
HE UNLEASHED THE FULL FORCE OF HIS CELEBRITY AGAINST ***FRANCE*** HERSELF, SPEAKING OUT CONSTANTLY AGAINST THE ***ALGERIAN WAR***!

IN 1961, ***5,000*** FRENCH VETERANS MARCHED THROUGH THE CHAMPS-ELYSEES, SHOUTING:
SHOOT SARTRE!
SARTRE: NON!
RIGHT-WINGERS BOMBED HIS APARTMENT-- ***TWICE!***

IN 1964, THE ***NOBEL PRIZE COMMITTEE*** TRIED TO HONOR HIM WITH ITS ***LITERATURE*** AWARD...
...FOR ***TIRELESSLY*** CHAMPIONING THE CAUSE OF HUMAN ***FREEDOM...***
PASS!
...BUT HE ***REFUSED*** IT, SAYING HE DID NOT WANT TO BECOME "AN ***INSTITUTION***."

BUT IN MANY WAYS, HE ALREADY ***WAS*** -- THE EPITOME OF THE ***ACTIVIST-INTELLECTUAL***!
SARTRE WAS THAT ***RAREST*** OF THINKERS -- ONE WHO FULLY ***EMBODIED*** HIS OWN PHILOSOPHY!
≠
PHILOSOPHY
->SIGH!<-
BEING & NOTHINGNESS
BEING & NOTHI
JEAN- SARTR

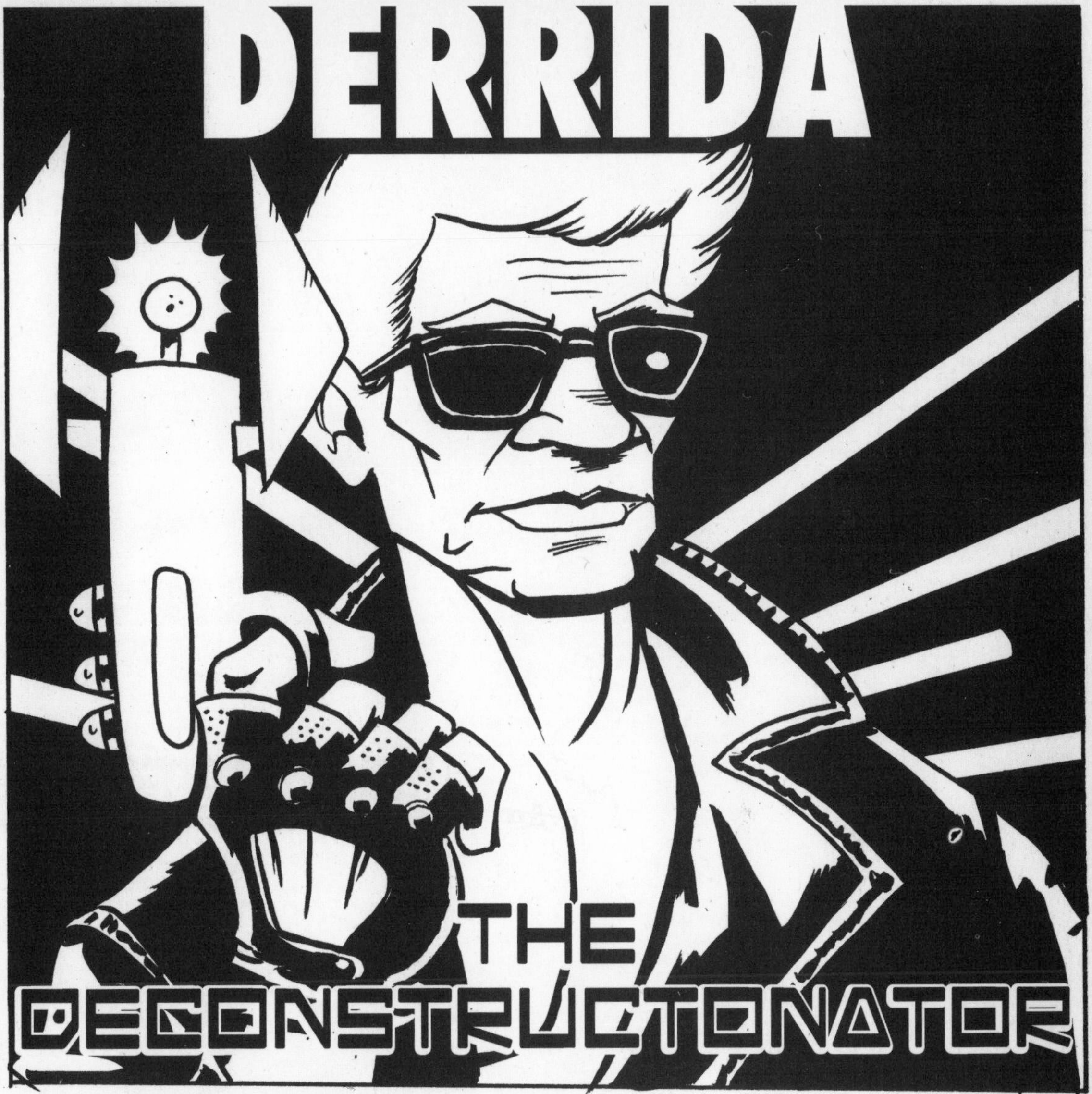

DERRIDA

THE DECONSTRUCTONATOR

HE SAYS, "WITH ALL THE JEWISH PROFESSORS THAT HAD BEEN FIRED, IT WAS EASY TO RECONSTITUTE A REALLY GOOD (JEWISH) SCHOOL. I DIDN'T LIKE THIS SCHOOL EITHER."
Jews Rule!!
BLAH BLAH MOSES BLAH
THIS SUCKS TOO!
"THESE WERE THE YEARS THAT VERY MUCH COUNTED FOR ME. I WAS VERY MARKED OF SUFFERING BOTH FROM ANTI-SEMITISM AND MY OWN DISCOMFORT IN THE JEWISH COMMUNITY!"
ADRIFT BETWEEN TWO POLES, NEVER WHOLLY SATISFIED WITH ONE OR THE OTHER...
FORM
REALITY
CHIPS
Dasein
not Dasein
MIND
BODY
...IS IT ANY WONDER THAT LITTLE JACQUES GREW INTO A PHILOSOPHER OBSESSED WITH PUTTING STRESS ON THE DUALITIES THAT HAVE TRADITIONALLY DOMINATED WESTERN THOUGHT?
CAPITALIST
PROLETARIAT
DERRIDA FIRST GAINED NOTORIETY IN 1966, AS YOUNG TURKS OFTEN DO...
SEMIOTICS
...BY TAKING ON A SEEMINGLY UNASSAILABLE TARGET-- SWISS LINGUIST FERDINAND DE SAUSSURE (1857-1913)!
SAUSSURE, THE FOUNDER OF STRUCTURALIST LINGUISTICS (A.K.A. SEMIOTICS), ASSERTED SPEECH WAS SUPERIOR TO WRITING BECAUSE THE LATTER WAS MERELY A REPRESENTATION OF THE FORMER!
-SOB!- WHAT DOES SHE HAVE THAT I DON'T HAVE?
abc
(WRITING VS. SPEECH: HMMM, THERE'S ANOTHER OF THOSE PESKY DUALISMS!)

DERRIDA **REJECTED** THIS DISTINCTION, ARGUING THAT ALL **SIGNAGE**--SPEECH AS WELL AS WRITING--ENGAGES IN A PROCESS OF **INFINITE REFERRAL!**
PRECISE **MEANING?** NOT **MY** JOB. YOU WANNA TALK TO **HIM.**
NAW, FOR THAT YOU GOT TO GO TO MY **SUPERVISOR.**
I DON'T GOTS MY **CERTIFICATION** FOR THAT. SEE THE **DISTRICT HEAD.**
WHAAAAA? NO, YOU NEED OUR **REGIONAL CENTRAL MANAGER.**
WRITING
SPEECH
SIGNIFIER
SIGNIFIED
HE'S ON **VACATION,** THOUGH, WON'T BE BACK 'TIL **MONDAY...**

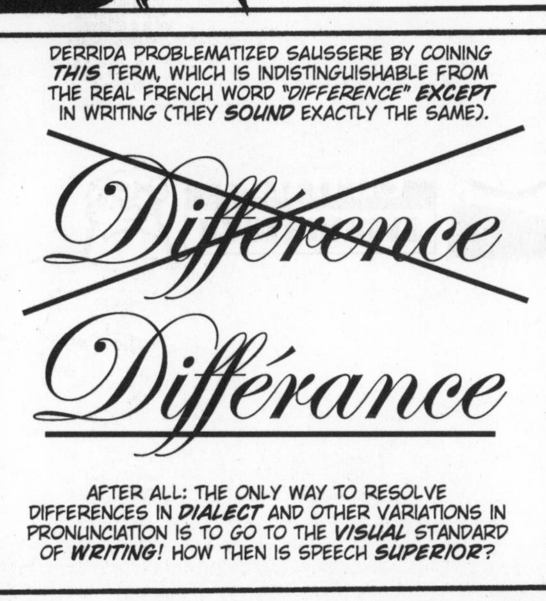
DERRIDA PROBLEMATIZED SAUSSERE BY COINING **THIS** TERM, WHICH IS INDISTINGUISHABLE FROM THE REAL FRENCH WORD **"DIFFERENCE" EXCEPT** IN WRITING (THEY **SOUND** EXACTLY THE SAME).
Différence
Différance
AFTER ALL: THE ONLY WAY TO RESOLVE DIFFERENCES IN **DIALECT** AND OTHER VARIATIONS IN PRONUNCIATION IS TO GO TO THE **VISUAL** STANDARD OF **WRITING!** HOW THEN IS SPEECH **SUPERIOR?**

DERRIDA WOULD SPEND HIS CAREER **EMPOWERING** THE SUBORDINATED HALVES OF DUALISMS!
abc
I AM **WRITING!** HEAR ME **ROAR!**
OHHHHHH....

REALITY
DECONSTRUCTION **"DESTRUCTIVELY RETRIEVES"** THE INHERENT **INSTABILITY** OF PHILOSOPHICAL TEXTS!
HIS METHOD, POPULARLY KNOWN AS **"DECONSTRUCTION"** (THOUGH THE TERM MADE **HIM** UNCOMFORTABLE), WAS TO EXPOSE THE PARADOXICAL PURSUIT OF **IMPOSSIBLE ABSOLUTES.**
TAKE HUSSERL'S **PHENOMENOLOGY,** FOR EXAMPLE...
OWWW!!! DO WE **HAVE** TO?

ITS DUALISM PRIVILIGES EACH PSYCHE'S EXPERIENTIAL "NOW" OVER THE PAST AND THE PRESENT--AND THE OBJECTIVE WORLD!
ONLY BY "BRACKETING" (GREEK=EPOCHE) ANYTHING BEYOND MY IMMEDIATE EXPERIENCE CAN I REFLECT ON THE ORIGINAL MODE OF EXISTENCE...
...MY LIFE, AS IT IS LIVED, MOMENT-TO-MOMENT!
FATHER TIME

NOT SO FAST, DERRIDA SAYS!
IS IT POSSIBLE TO EXPERIENCE ONLY THE PRESENT?
BZAP!

AFTER ALL, WE REFERENCE ALL OF OUR CURRENT EXPERIENCES AGAINST WHAT'S HAPPENED TO US IN THE PAST...
...AND THERE'S NO WAY TO APPRECIATE OUR PRESENT, EXCEPT BY LOOKING BACK FROM THE FUTURE...

...THEREFORE, BY HUSSERL'S OWN LOGIC, THE "IMMEDIATELY REFLECTIVE SELF" CANNOT EXIST!
HASTA LA VISTA, EPOCHE!
POIT!

FOR DERRIDA, NOTHING IS -- OR CAN EVER BE -- DEFINITE! THE "I" OF THE SELF IS ALWAYS IN THE PROCESS OF BECOMING -- CAUGHT IN THE SPACE BETWEEN THE TWIN POLES OF A DUALISM!
OPTION #1
OPTION 2
DERRIDA'S IS OFTEN CALLED "THE PHILOSOPHY OF HESITATION!"

THAT'S BETTER, THOUGH, THAN WHAT HE CALLS A "METAPHYSICS OF PRESENCE"--
-SIGH!- MY HERO!
-- THE NOSTALGIC DELUSION OF MOST PHILOSOPHERS TO PRIVILEGE AN "IS" THAT SIMPLY CANNOT BE!

THE BIGGEST PARADOX OF PHILOSOPHY IS THAT IF IT EVER ACHIEVED IRREFUTABLE MEANING BY SOLVING ITS MYRIAD OF HIGH-FALUTIN' PROBLEMS, IT WOULD CEASE TO EXIST!
16 TONS
OPTION #2
YES! I MADE IT!
OPTION #1

NOTHING MORE TO DEBATE -- NOTHING MORE TO PONDER -- IT WOULD DELIVER A COMPLETE SELF-EVIDENT "SYSTEM", HERE AND NOW!
PHILOSOPHY 2.0
THE TRUE END OF PHILOSOPHY IS THE END OF PHILOSOPHY!

FOR THE BETTER PART OF FOUR DECADES DERRIDA CRANKED OUT BOOK-LENGTH DECONSTRUCTIONS OF DESCARTES, FREUD, MARX, AND MANY OTHERS...
WORKER! AND...CAPITALIST? YOU TWO...ARE... TOGETHER?!?
YOU CAN'T HANDLE THE TRUTH!!
...DEMONSTRATING, AS IN THE CASE OF THE PHENOMENOLOGICAL EPOCHE, THAT EACH POLE OF A THINKER'S DUALISM CONTAINS A "TRACE" OF ITS OTHER!

TO SAY THIS MADE DERRIDA A CONTROVERSIAL FIGURE AMONG TRADITIONAL PHILOSOPHERS WOULD BE A CONSIDERABLE UNDERSTATEMENT.
PHILOSOPHY
AND STAY OUT!!
TOSS!
HE WAS DENOUNCED AS A GIMMICKY CHARLATAN BY MANY --
DECONSTRUCTION DISMISSED AS THE "PHILOSOPHY ABOUT NOTHING" (THIS WAS BACK WHEN SEINFELD WAS BIG)--

PAGE SIX

PANEL 6: CLOSE UP ON DERRIDA

DERRIDA: In order to be FAITHFUL to a text's true meaning we must invent NEW ONES for it!

DERRIDA: "Invent in your OWN language if you can or want to hear MINE; invent if you can or want to give my language to be understood."

DERRIDA: Any faithful INTERPRETATION of my work would require a student to go BEYOND it!

RYAN! WHAT THE HELL WAS THAT?
OUR COMIC BOOK IS STARTING TO BREAK DOWN, FRED!
ACTION PHILOSOPHER

OUR GRAMMATOLOGICAL SHIELDS ARE FAILING--
THIS STORY IS BEING HIJACKED BY AN ALTERNATE READING--

ZAP!
I AM ALWAYS ALREADY BACK!
AAHHH! DERRIDA! AAHHH!

WHAT CAN WE DO? WHAT CAN WE DO?
GET TO THE AUTHORIAL DRIVE! IF HE DESTRUCTIVELY RETRIEVES OUR PARADOXIUM WE'RE SUNK!
ZAP!

CRAP ON A CRACKER!! THAT CONTRADICTION FUELS OUR ENTIRE PROJECT!
AUTHORIAL DRIVE
ACTION PHILOSOPHER
TELL ME ABOUT IT! THIS BOOK IS BILLED AS AN OBJECTIVE EXPLICATION OF PHILOSOPHICAL CONCEPTS THRU COMICS!
BUT THE IMPOSITION OF MY WORDS AND YOUR DRAWINGS FUNDAMENTALLY TRANSMOGRIFIES OTHERS' IDEAS INTO A THIRD, WHOLLY SEPARATE ENTITY!

COULD THIS BE THE *END* OF *ACTION PHILOSOPHERS*?

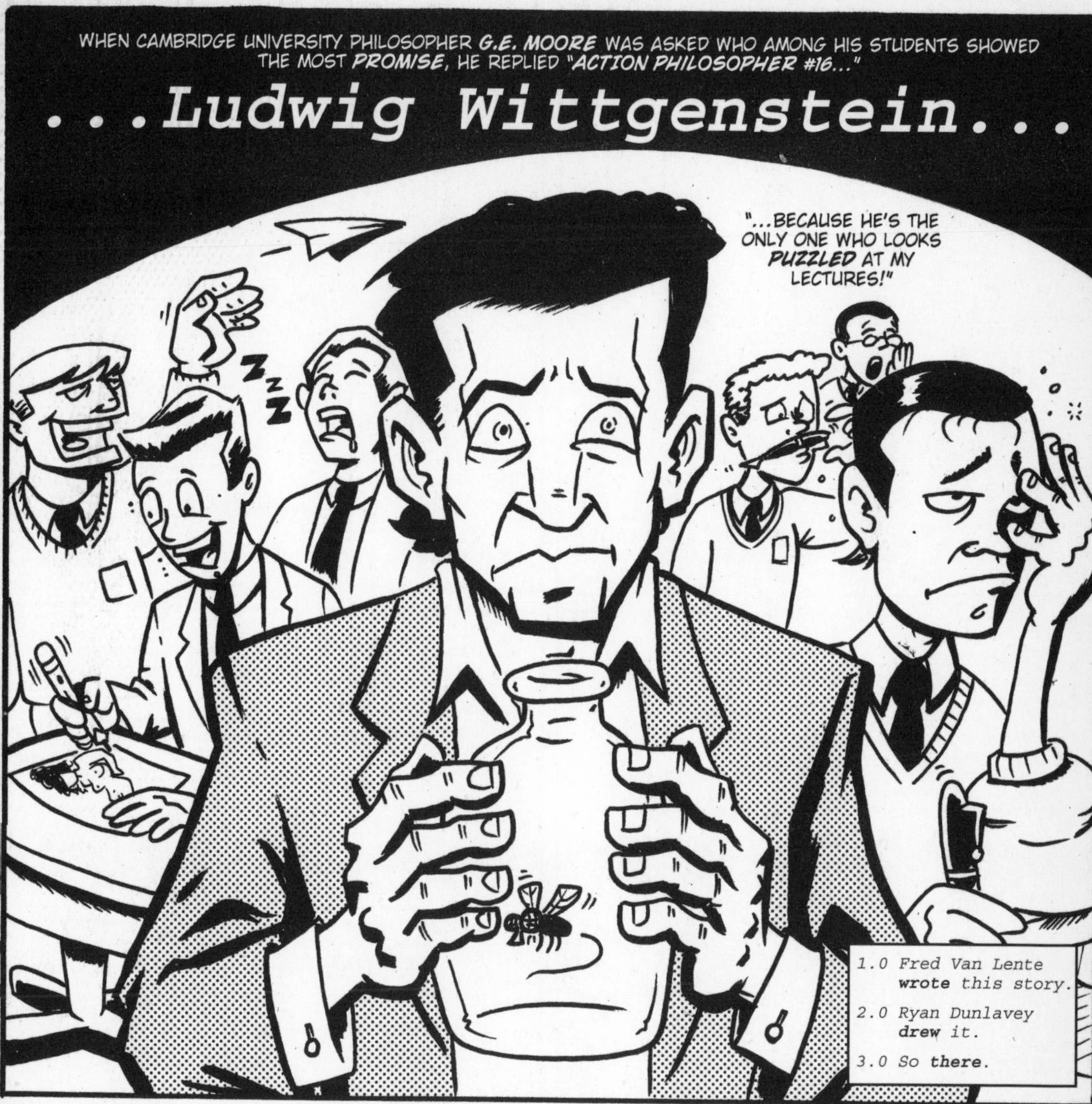

WHEN CAMBRIDGE UNIVERSITY PHILOSOPHER ***G.E. MOORE*** WAS ASKED WHO AMONG HIS STUDENTS SHOWED THE MOST ***PROMISE***, HE REPLIED "***ACTION PHILOSOPHER #16...***"

...Ludwig Wittgenstein...

"...BECAUSE HE'S THE ONLY ONE WHO LOOKS ***PUZZLED*** AT MY LECTURES!"

1.0 Fred Van Lente **wrote** this story.
2.0 Ryan Dunlavey **drew** it.
3.0 So **there**.

RUSSELL DEMANDED THAT PHILOSOPHY TAKE THE FORM OF ***PROPOSITIONS*** THAT PRECISELY REFLECT ***REALITY***.

HIS ***LOGICALLY PERFECT LANGUAGE*** WOULD REMOVE ALL ***AMBIGUITY*** BY REDUCING FACTS TO THEIR ***SIMPLEST COMPONENTS***.

The King of France is bald.

THIS STATEMENT MIGHT ***SEEM*** SIMPLE ON ITS ***FACE***...

...BUT ***ACTUALLY*** IT CAN BE BROKEN DOWN INTO ITS COMPONENT "***ATOMIC FACTS!***"

1.0 There **is** a King of France.
2.0 There is only **one** King of France.
3.0 Whatever is King of France is **bald**.

RUSSELL BELIEVED ***ALL*** LOGICAL AND PHILOSOPHICAL PROBLEMS SHOULD BE EXPRESSED IN CHAINS OF ***ATOMIC FACTS*** -- OR "***MOLECULAR PROPOSITIONS!***"

EVER THE EFFICIENT ***MATHEMATICIAN***, RUSSELL EVEN DEVELOPED ***LOGICAL NOTATION*** STILL USED TODAY; THE PROPOSITION IN THE PREVIOUS PANEL CAN ALSO BE EXPRESSED AS:

$$(\exists x)\ [Fx\ \&\ (y)\ (Fy \rightarrow y=x)\ \&\ Gx]$$

(UH... JUST DON'T ASK US ***WHY.***)

LUKI ***EMBODIED*** THE SUCCINCT CLARITY OF HIS TEACHER. ONCE, AT A 1912 MEETING OF CAMBRIDGE'S ***MORAL SCIENCE CLUB:***

DID WE SAY "EMBODIED?" ACCORDING TO RUSSELL, LUKI SURPASSED HIM, EVEN AS AN UNDERGRADUATE:
SEEING YOU WORK MAKES ME REALIZE I WILL NEVER AGAIN DO FUNDAMENTAL WORK IN PHILOSOPHY!
YOU WILL SOLVE ALL THE PROBLEMS I AM TOO OLD TO!

LUKI'S GENIUS WAS A PRETTY GOOD ARGUMENT AGAINST BALANCE IN NATURE.
CANDY SHOPPE
HE ALREADY CAME FROM ONE OF EUROPE'S WEALTHIEST FAMILIES; HIS FATHER KARL CONTROLLED AUSTRIA'S STEEL CARTEL!

DESPITE HIS VAST FORTUNE AND BRAINS, LUKI WAS VERY MUCH A PRODUCT OF AUSTRIA'S ANCIENT WARRIOR CULTURE.
WHEN WORLD WAR ONE BROKE OUT, HE VOLUNTEERED FOR THE ARMY AND WAS DECORATED MULTIPLE TIMES AS A FORWARD ARTILLERY OBSERVER!

THE WAR CHANGED LUKI. AFTER HE WAS RELEASED FROM AN ITALIAN P.O.W. CAMP IN 1919, HE LITERALLY GAVE AWAY HIS INHERITED MILLIONS TO HIS SIBLINGS.
APPARENTLY DECIDING TO LIVE OUT THE SIMPLE CLARITY OF HIS PHILOSOPHY, HE BECAME A PUBLIC SCHOOL TEACHER IN AUSTRIA'S POOREST RURAL AREAS!

THIS MAYBE WASN'T THE WISEST CAREER CHOICE FOR SOMEONE WITH LUKI'S TEMPERAMENT.
SCHOOL
HE HAD TO QUIT IN 1926 AFTER GETTING HAULED INTO COURT FOR SMACKING ONE OF HIS SICKLIER STUDENTS UNCONSCIOUS!

LUKI RETURNED TO VIENNA, WHERE HE WORKED FOR A TIME AS A GARDENER, AND DESIGNED A SUMMER HOME FOR HIS SISTER. HE HAD NO PLANS TO RETURN TO PHILOSOPHY.
NOK!
NOK!
BUT THEN, IN 1927...
H-H-HERR WITTGENSTEIN?
YEAH?
H-H-HERR LUDWIG JOSEF JOHANN WITTGENSTEIN?
YEAH.
HERR WITTGENSTEIN, AUTHOR OF THE TRACTATUS LOGICO-PHILOSOPHICUS?
YEAH!
UH...
YEAH?
M-M-MY NAME IS MORITZ SCHLICK. I T-T-TEACH PHILOSOPHY AT THE UNIVERSITY?
B-B-BEHIND ME IS THE VIENNA CIRCLE...
... AND WE'RE NOT WORTHY!!
!?!
LUKI HAD ALL BUT FORGOTTEN THE ONE BOOK HE WOULD PUBLISH IN HIS LIFETIME, WITH RUSSELL'S HELP, BACK IN 1921...
...BUT, WITHOUT HIS KNOWLEDGE, THE TRACTATUS HAD BEEN ADOPTED AS THE BIBLE OF SCHLICK'S CIRCLE, A LOCAL SOCIETY OF MATHEMATICIANS, SCIENTISTS AND PHILOSOPHERS...
...WHICH HAD ALREADY SPENT A YEAR READING IT OUT LOUD AND DISCUSSING IT, SENTENCE BY SENTENCE... TWICE!
TRACTATUS LOGICO-PHILOSOPHICUS
THE VIENNA CIRCLE TOOK RUSSELL'S CONTEMPT FOR METAPHYSICS ONE STEP FURTHER...

IN LUKI'S *TRACTATUS* THE VIENNA CIRCLE THOUGHT THEY FOUND THE PERFECT **RULEBOOK** TO GUIDE THEM THROUGH CONSISTENT APPLICATION OF THEIR ***VERIFICATION PRINCIPLE***.

2 What is the case--a fact--is the existence of states of affairs.

2.1 We make to ourselves pictures of facts.

2.13 To the objects correspond in the picture the elements of the picture.

2.131 The elements of the picture stand, in the picture, for the objects.

THE BOOK IS A ARRANGED IN A SERIES OF SIMPLE, HIERARCHICAL--***MOLECULAR***--PROPOSITIONS, NUMBERED IN THEIR ORDER OF IMPORTANCE TO EACH OTHER.

WE HUMBLY SUGGEST THAT LUKI ENVISIONED THE T.L.P. BEING USED IN THIS WAY:
WELCOME TO MONDAY NIGHT PHILOSOPHY, COMING TO YOU LIVE FROM THANATOS STADIUM!
TONIGHT IT'S A METAPHYSICAL CONFERENCE GRUDGE MATCH BETWEEN TWO BITTER RIVALS...
...THE MIDWEST GODBOYS AND THE LEFT COAST'S DOUBTING TOMS!
TONIGHT THESE TWO TEAMS WILL BE TUSSLING FOR POSSESSION OF ONE OF THE BIGGEST PIGSKINS OF ALL:
"IS THERE LIFE AFTER DEATH?"
666
WILL THE GODBOYS' LEAGUE-LEADING DEFENSE WITHSTAND THE TOMS' ATHEISTIC OFFENSIVE LINE?
AS ALWAYS, THE REFS WILL BE GUIDED BY WITTGENSTEIN'S TRACTATUS...
...THE BOOK THAT, AS ITS AUTHOR WROTE, "DRAWS A LIMIT...TO THE EXPRESSION OF THOUGHTS."
THIS LIMIT IS THAT OF LANGUAGE-- WORDS REPRESENT PICTURES THAT REFLECT FACTS IN THE WORLD, AS PER PROPOSITION 2.1511:
"THUS THE PICTURE IS LINKED WITH REALITY; IT REACHES UP TO IT."
ROSE
5.6: "THE LIMITS OF MY LANGUAGE MEAN THE LIMITS OF MY WORLD!"
6.13: "LOGIC IS NOT A THEORY BUT A REFLECTION OF THE WORLD!"
stink weed ≠
THEREFORE, ALL LANGUAGE THAT DOES NOT LITERALLY REFLECT REALITY IS NONSENSE!

TWEEEE!!
WHOA NELLY!! GET A LOAD O' THIS!! THE REF IS ALREADY CALLING A NONSENSE PENALTY!!!
WELL, THIS I GOTTA HEAR...
GODBOY
3
66

VIOLATION. PROP. 6.4311:
DEATH IS NOT AN EVENT OF LIFE.
DEATH IS NOT LIVED THROUGH.
666
3

OUR LIFE IS ENDLESS IN THE WAY THAT OUR VISUAL FIELD IS WITHOUT LIMIT.
THEREFORE, ON ITS FACE, THE QUESTION "IS THERE LIFE AFTER DEATH?" IS NONSENSE!
GAME OVER!

LUKI DECLARED THAT HIS TRACTATUS HAD SOLVED ALL THE PROBLEMS OF PHILOSOPHY...
...IF BY "SOLVED" YOU MEAN HE DECLARED THE VAST MAJORITY OF THEM NULL AND VOID.
PROP. 4.0031: "ALL PHILOSOPHY IS 'CRITIQUE OF LANGUAGE.'"
EXIT
666
3
18

PROP. 6.5: "FOR AN ANSWER WHICH *CANNOT* BE EXPRESSED THE QUESTION *TOO* CANNOT BE EXPRESSED!"

"IF A QUESTION *CAN* BE PUT AT ALL, THEN IT CAN *ALSO BE ANSWERED*!"

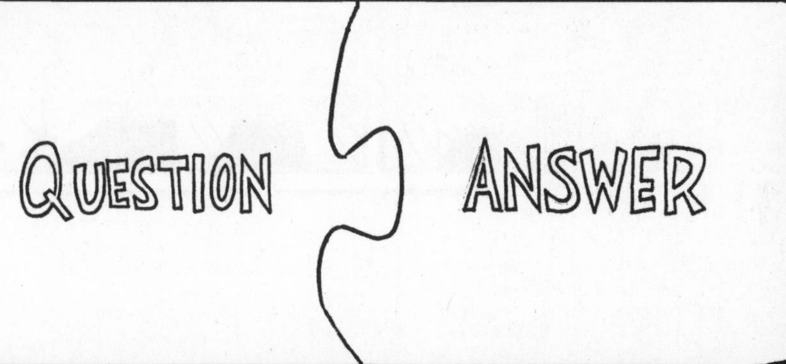

"THE RIDDLE *DOES NOT EXIST*."

5.1361! "THE EVENTS OF THE FUTURE *CANNOT* BE INFERRED FROM THOSE OF THE PRESENT!"
6.36311! "THAT THE SUN WILL RISE TOMORROW IS AN *HYPOTHESIS*; AND THAT MEANS THAT WE DO NOT *KNOW* WHETHER IT WILL RISE!"

THE LOGICAL POSITIVISTS' TIME IN THE PHILOSOPHICAL SUN WOULD BE *BRIEF*, DUE TO THE *TOTAL DISCREDITING* OF THEIR *VERIFICATION PRINCIPLE*.

NEVERTHELESS, LUKI'S ENCOUNTER WITH THE VIENNA CIRCLE APPEARED TO SPARK HIS INTEREST IN PHILOSOPHY *ANEW*.

IN 1929 HE DECIDED TO RETURN TO *CAMBRIDGE*. HE CONTACTED HIS OLD *PROFESSORS*, RUSSELL AND MOORE.
HUH. *WITTGENSTEIN* WANTS A *DOCTORATE*.
WHAT'S HIS *DISSERTATION*?

THE *TRACTATUS LOGICO-PHILOSOPHICUS*...
...THE MOST *INFLUENTIAL WORK OF PHILOSOPHY* OF THE EARLY 20TH CENTURY.

FLIP!

FLIP!

FLIP!

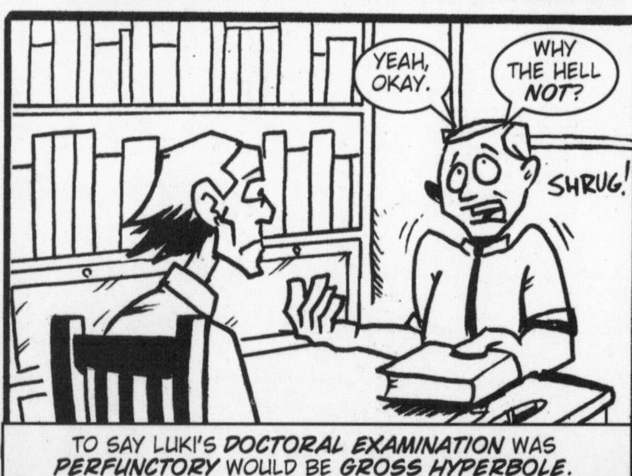
YEAH, OKAY.
WHY THE HELL *NOT*?
SHRUG!
TO SAY LUKI'S *DOCTORAL EXAMINATION* WAS *PERFUNCTORY* WOULD BE *GROSS HYPERBOLE*.

DOCTOR LUKI SPENT MOST OF THE REST OF HIS LIFE TEACHING AT CAMBRIDGE.
HIS STUDENTS FOUND HIM TO BE A CHARISMATIC, MESMERIZING FIGURE...

...NOT THAT HIS TEMPERAMENT HAD CHANGED FROM HIS ELEMENTARY SCHOOL TEACHING DAYS:
THERE'S NOTHING MORE USELESS THAN A PROFESSIONAL PHILOSOPHER!
ALL REAL PHILOSOPHERS SHOULD BECOME BRICKLAYERS, OR SOME OTHER KIND OF MANUAL LABORER! WORKING WITH ONE'S HANDS IS GOOD FOR THE MIND!*
*: ACTUAL QUOTE!

HE WAS NO MORE FORGIVING OF HIMSELF, ULTIMATELY DENOUNCING HIS OWN TRACTATUS AS FATALLY FLAWED!
abc
HE SAID HE HAD BEEN THE VICTIM, LIKE EVERYONE ELSE, OF "THE BEWITCHMENT OF OUR INTELLIGENCE BY MEANS OF LANGUAGE!"

THE IDEA THAT LANGUAGE REPRESENTS PICTURES IS A "GRAMMATICAL ILLUSION" PRODUCED BY THOUGHT:
"THERE IS A TENDENCY ROOTED IN OUR USUAL FORMS OF EXPRESSION-- SAY, THE TERM 'LEAF'--"
ROSE

"--TO THINK THAT THE MAN WHO HAS LEARNT TO UNDERSTAND A GENERAL TERM HAS THEREBY COME TO POSSESS A KIND OF GENERAL PICTURE OF A LEAF..."
"...AS OPPOSED TO PICTURES OF PARTICULAR LEAVES."

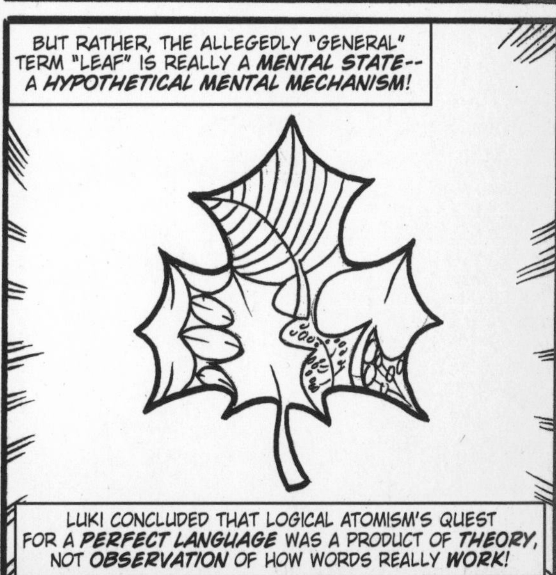
BUT RATHER, THE ALLEGEDLY "GENERAL" TERM "LEAF" IS REALLY A MENTAL STATE-- A HYPOTHETICAL MENTAL MECHANISM!
LUKI CONCLUDED THAT LOGICAL ATOMISM'S QUEST FOR A PERFECT LANGUAGE WAS A PRODUCT OF THEORY, NOT OBSERVATION OF HOW WORDS REALLY WORK!

LOOK AT THE WORD "GAME"-- WHICH DESCRIBES ALL OF THE ACTIVITIES/OBJECTS BELOW ...
BUT, WHILE THEY MAY BEAR A FEW "FAMILY LIKENESSES," REALLY, THESE THINGS HAVE NOTHING AT ALL TO DO WITH EACH OTHER!
WORDS CANNOT HAVE JUST ONE FORM--REFER TO ONE PICTURE-- THEY ARE AS VARIED AS LIFE ITSELF!
25¢
LUKI: "CRAVING FOR GENERALITY... LEADS THE PHILOSOPHER INTO COMPLETE DARKNESS!"
TAKE A COMMON PHILOSOPHICAL "RIDDLE" OF THE DAY:
WE'VE ALREADY ALLUDED TO WHAT HUME CALLED THE PROBLEM OF INDUCTION.
I.E., WHEN AN ARGUMENT SUPPORTS A CONCLUSION WITHOUT ENSURING IT.
THAT IS TO SAY, JUST BECAUSE YOU'VE OBSERVED GRAVITY WORK IN THE PAST, THAT DOESN'T MEAN IT WILL ALWAYS WORK IN THE FUTURE.
WHEW! I'M LUCKY I STUDIED PHILOSOPHY AND NOT LAW!
(THE LAW OF GRAVITY, THAT IS...)
THEREFORE, OR SO THIS CONUNDRUM GOES...
...WHY, LOGICALLY, SHOULDN'T YOU JUMP OFF THE EIFFEL TOWER?

BECAUSE I DON'T ***WANT*** TO!!

WHAT KIND OF A **MORON** WANTS TO JUMP OFF THE EIFFEL TOWER?!

THIS IS **EXACTLY** THE KIND OF POINTLESS MUMBO-JUMBO I'M **TALKING** ABOUT!!

ERROR RESULTS WHEN LANGUAGE IS ***IDLING*** (I.E., ***DEFINING***) RATHER THAN ***WORKING*** (I.E., ***DESCRIBING***)!

EMPHASIS

TWIST

ENLIGHTEN

DIVIDE

LUKI'S NEW ***"ORDINARY LANGUAGE PHILOSOPHY"*** REJECTED GENERALITIES AND USED WORDS AS THEY WERE ***MEANT*** TO BE USED--AS ***TOOLS***--WITHIN CONTEXT OF ***EACH OTHER***!

"WHAT WE DO IS TO BRING WORDS ***BACK*** FROM THEIR METAPHYSICAL TO THEIR ***EVERYDAY*** USAGE!"

"A PHILOSOPHICAL PROBLEM HAS THE FORM: 'I DON'T KNOW MY WAY ***ABOUT***.'"

OUR JOB IS TO "SHOW THE FLY THE WAY ***OUT*** OF THE FLY-BOTTLE!"

AND SO WITTGENSTEIN HAS THE DISTINCTION OF BEING THE ***ONLY*** PHILOSOPHER IN HISTORY TO HAVE DEFINED ***TWO*** (*COUNT 'EM! TWO!*) WHOLLY ***SEPARATE*** AND ***MUTUALLY EXCLUSIVE*** SCHOOLS OF THOUGHT!

HOW DO YOU ***FEEL*** ABOUT THAT, LUKI?

3

666

CAN'T TALK NOW. ***THINKING***.

ER...OKAY...WE'LL CHECK BACK IN WITH YOU ***LATER***...

LOOK OUT, ATHEISTS!!

HERE COMES *THREE HUNDRED POUNDS* OF THEOLOGICAL THAUMATURGY...

THAT *PEERLESS PACHYDERM* OF *PIOUS POSTULATING*...

THE MAN THEY CALL THE *"SCHOLASTIC SPASTIC"*...

(...AND ACTION PHILOSOPHER #17:)

SIR McD'S

DAME WENDY

KAMELOT FRIED CHICKEN

BURGER LIEGE

ON THE CONTRARY,
FRED VAN LENTE, HE *WRITETH*,
AND RYAN DUNLAVEY, HE DOTH *DRAW*.

St. Thomas Aquinas!

Fear NOT Thomas! God has HEARD thy prayers and sent US to help thee!

Did not a HOLY MAN on the hour of thy birth predict that NO ONE would be found to equal to thy LEARNING and thy SANCTITY?

We GIRD THEE with the girdle of PERPETUAL VIRGINITY!

AWESOME! GOD'S THE ***BEST!***

Yes. We know. We're ANGELS.

-HEH, HEH!- ONCE THAT WILY STRUMPET STAINS THOMAS'S CHASTITY BEYOND REDEMPTION, THE DOMINICANS WILL HAVE NO CHOICE BUT TO BOOT HIS ASS RIGHT OUT OF THE ORDER!
THEN HE'LL BE FREE TO BECOME THE BISHOP OR CARDINAL I ALWAYS WANTED...
FAT VATICAN CONTRACTS, HERE I COME...
EEEEEEEEEE!!
BACK TO THE DEPTHS OF THE INFERNO WITH YOU, HELLSPAWN!!
THOMAS'S PARENTS HELD HIM IN CAPTIVITY FOR NEARLY TWO YEARS.
FINALLY, AROUND 1245, THE COUNTESS PERSUADED HER HUSBAND TO LET THEIR SON FOLLOW WHAT HE CLEARLY SAW AS GOD'S WILL.
HE WAS LOWERED DOWN TO HIS BROTHER MONKS IN A BASKET.
SPLAT!
(WE CAN ONLY ASSUME THE BASKET WAS THE COUNT'S IDEA.)
THE DOMINICANS DISCOVERED THOMAS HAD SPENT HIS IMPRISONMENT STUDYING, SO THEY SENT HIM TO PARIS, THE CENTER OF LEARNING OF THE MEDIEVAL WORLD.
MANY OF HIS TEACHERS MISTOOK HIS EXTREME HUMILITY FOR DULLNESS, CALLING HIM A "DUMB OX", BUT LEGENDARY THEOLOGIAN ALBERT THE GREAT RECOGNIZED:
THAT "DUMB OX'S" BELLOWING IN DOCTRINE WILL ONE DAY RESOUND THROUGHOUT THE WORLD!

ALBERT BELIEVED THAT FAITH SHOULD BE MARRIED TO ***REASON*** WHENEVER POSSIBLE!

HE LED THE ***"SCHOLASTIC"*** MOVEMENT THAT FUSED CHRISTIAN TEACHINGS WITH THE NEWLY-TRANSLATED (INTO ***LATIN***) SECULAR PHILOSOPHIES OF ***ARISTOTLE***!

WHEN THOMAS BEGAN TEACHING IN PARIS ***HIMSELF*** IN ***1252***, HE WAS OPPOSED, AT FIRST, BY ***PLATONISTS*** (LIKE ***ST. BONAVENTURA***) WHO FELT ARISTOTLE'S ***REJECTION*** OF THE THEORY OF FORMS DENIED THAT GOD POSSESSED ALL THE ***IDEAS*** OF THE WORLD!

THOMAS SET ABOUT ***"CHRISTIANIZING"*** ARISTOTLE TO MAKE HIM FIT FOR USE IN THE ***THEOLOGICAL*** CLASSROOM!

HE WROTE IN CAREFULLY-CONSTRUCTED ***DIALECTICS*** THAT EXEMPLIFIED THE CLEAR, SIMPLE STRUCTURE OF ARISTOTELIAN ***LOGIC***:

QUESTION: Whether God exists?

Proof the First: from MOTION

FOR MOTION IS NOTHING ELSE THAN THE REDUCTION OF SOMETHING FROM *POTENTIALITY* TO *ACTUALITY*.

POTENTIAL ACTUAL

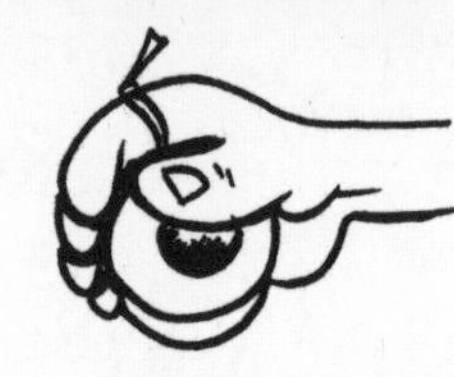

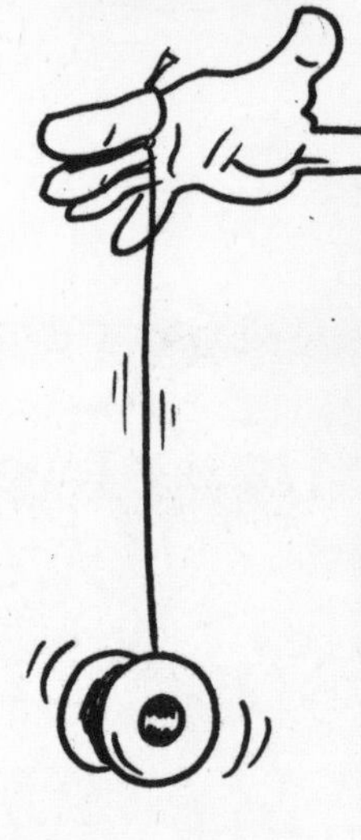

BUT *NOTHING* CAN BE REDUCED FROM POTENTIALITY TO ACTUALITY, EXCEPT BY SOMETHING *IN* A STATE OF ACTUALITY!

IT IS THEREFORE *IMPOSSIBLE* THAT A THING SHOULD BE MOVER *AND* MOVED, *I.E.* THAT IT SHOULD MOVE *ITSELF*!

IF THAT BY WHICH IT IS PUT IN MOTION BE *ITSELF* PUT IN MOTION, THEN THIS *ALSO* MUST NEEDS BE PUT IN MOTION BY ANOTHER, AND THAT BY ANOTHER *AGAIN*...

...BUT THIS CANNOT GO ON TO *INFINITY*, BECAUSE THEN THERE WOULD BE NO *FIRST* MOVER, AND, CONSEQUENTLY NO *OTHER* MOVER.

Proof the Second: from
EFFICIENT CAUSE
THERE IS NO CASE KNOWN (NEITHER IS IT, INDEED, POSSIBLE)...
...IN WHICH A THING IS FOUND TO BE THE EFFICIENT CAUSE OF ITSELF; FOR SO IT WOULD BE PRIOR TO ITSELF, WHICH IS IMPOSSIBLE.
!?!?!
NOW IN EFFICIENT CAUSES IT IS NOT POSSIBLE TO GO ON TO INFINITY, BECAUSE IN ALL EFFICIENT CAUSES FOLLOWING IN ORDER, THE FIRST IS THE CAUSE OF THE INTERMEDIATE CAUSE...
3 2 1
...AND THE INTERMEDIATE CAUSE IS THE CAUSE OF THE ULTIMATE CAUSE, WHETHER THE INTERMEDIATE CAUSE BE SEVERAL, OR ONE ONLY.
NOW TO TAKE AWAY THE CAUSE IS TO TAKE AWAY THE EFFECT!
3 2 1
THEREFORE, IF THERE BE NO FIRST CAUSE AMONG EFFICIENT CAUSES, THERE WILL BE NO ULTIMATE, NOR ANY INTERMEDIATE CAUSE.
BUT IF IN INFINITE CAUSES IT IS POSSIBLE TO GO ON TO INFINITY, THERE WILL BE NO FIRST EFFICIENT CAUSE, NEITHER WILL THERE BE AN ULTIMATE EFFECT-- WHICH IS PLAINLY FALSE!
THEREFORE IT IS NECESSARY TO ADMIT A FIRST EFFICIENT CAUSE...
...AND THIS EVERYONE UNDERSTANDS TO BE GOD!

Proof the Third: from NECESSARY vs. POSSIBLE BEING

Proof the Fourth: from the
DEGREES OF PERFECTION

Proof the Fifth: from the
ORDER of the
UNIVERSE
WE SEE THAT THINGS WHICH LACK INTELLIGENCE--
P. DIDDY
ER...
NO...
WE MEAN NATURAL BODIES...

...ACT FOR AN END, AND THIS IS EVIDENT FROM THEIR ACTING ALWAYS, OR NEARLY ALWAYS, IN THE SAME WAY, SO AS TO OBTAIN THE BEST RESULT.
"TOUCH OF CLASS" TRAILER PARK
REBEL
BEER

HENCE IT IS PLAIN THAT NOT FORTUITOUSLY, BUT DESIGNEDLY, DO THEY ACHIEVE THEIR END.
NOW WHATEVER LACKS INTELLIGENCE CANNOT MOVE TOWARDS AN END, UNLESS IT BE DIRECTED BY SOME BEING ENDOWED WITH KNOWLEDGE AND INTELLIGENCE...

...THEREFORE, SOME INTELLIGENT BEING EXISTS BY WHOM ALL NATURAL THINGS ARE DIRECTED TO THEIR END, AND THIS BEING WE CALL...
I @#$%&*! HATE TRAILER PARKS!!
...ER...YOU KNOW...

REPLY OBJ.: AS AUGUSTINE SAYS:
"SINCE GOD IS THE HIGHEST GOOD, HE WOULD NOT ALLOW ANY EVIL TO EXIST IN HIS WORKS...
...UNLESS HIS OMNIPOTENCE AND GOODNESS WERE SUCH AS TO BRING GOOD EVEN OUT OF EVIL!"
AAAHHHH! NO MORE! YOU WIN!

THOMAS WAS SO RIDICULOUSLY SUCCESSFUL AT SHOWING HOW THE METHODS OF THE PAGAN GREEKS COULD BE APPLIED TO CHRISTIAN THOUGHT THAT ARISTOTLE & CO. REMAIN THE FOUNDATION OF PHILOSOPHY THROUGHOUT CHRISTENDOM TO THIS DAY.

THANKS A BUNCH, AQUINAS-DUDE!
COLLEGE
ARISTOTLE'S POETICS

THOMAS SPENT THE REMAINDER OF HIS LIFE (D. 1274) PREACHING, WRITING, AND TEACHING.
CANONIZED IN 1323, HE IS THE PATRON SAINT OF CATHOLIC SCHOOLS AND UNIVERSITIES.

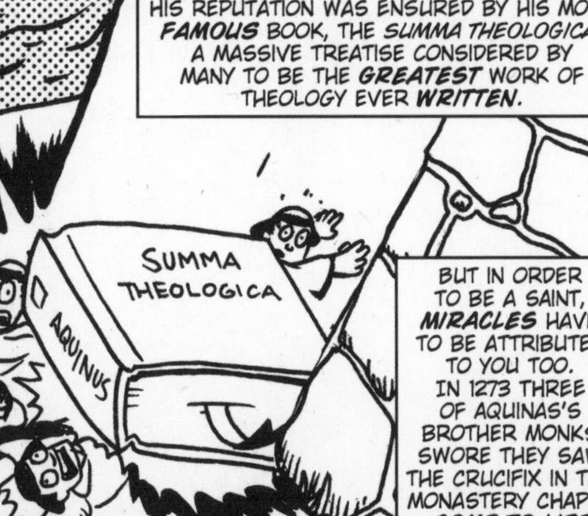
HIS REPUTATION WAS ENSURED BY HIS MOST FAMOUS BOOK, THE SUMMA THEOLOGICA, A MASSIVE TREATISE CONSIDERED BY MANY TO BE THE GREATEST WORK OF THEOLOGY EVER WRITTEN.
SUMMA THEOLOGICA
AQUINUS
BUT IN ORDER TO BE A SAINT, MIRACLES HAVE TO BE ATTRIBUTED TO YOU TOO. IN 1273 THREE OF AQUINAS'S BROTHER MONKS SWORE THEY SAW THE CRUCIFIX IN THE MONASTERY CHAPEL COME TO LIFE:

Thou hast written WELL of me Thomas; what REWARD wilt thou have?
NONE OTHER THAN THYSELF, LORD!
NOW HOW MANY PHILOSOPHERS CAN BOAST SUCH GLOWING REVIEWS BY THEIR OWN SUBJECTS?

IN 1855, AFTER REPEATED, VEHEMENT ATTACKS ON DENMARK'S STATE RELIGION, THE MOST POPULAR GUY IN COPENHAGEN WAS MOST DEFINITELY NOT ACTION PHILOSOPHER #18:
Søren Kierkegaard
BUT HE WAS HAVING THE TIME OF HIS LIFE!
WRITTEN (OUT OF FEAR) BY FRED VAN LENTE DRAWN (THOUGH TREMBLING) BY RYAN DUNLAVEY!
AH, HA! MY ARCH-NEMESIS, THE DANISH PEOPLE'S CHURCH!
I'VE GOT YOU RIGHT WHERE I WANT YOU!
AND I SWEAR TO YOU... I WILL HAVE THE LAST LAUGH!

THE CHURCH HAD AROUSED THE PHILOSOPHER'S IRE AT THE FUNERAL OF ITS BISHOP PRIMATE, J.P. MYNSTER.
FROM THIS MAN, WHOSE PRECIOUS MEMORY FILLS OUR HEARTS...
...OUR THOUGHTS ARE LED BACK TO THAT LONG LINE OF SANDHEDSVIDNE*...
* = "WITNESSES TO THE TRUTH" (DANISH)

...WHICH, LIKE A HOLY CHAIN, STRETCHES THROUGH TIME FROM THE APOSTLES UP TO OUR OWN DAY...
SANDHEDSVIDNE? SANDHEDSVIDNE?!
WHAT A RIP-OFF!!

THOUGH LARGELY UNKNOWN OUTSIDE HIS NATIVE LAND (HE WROTE IN DANISH, WHICH DIDN'T HELP), KIERKEGAARD WAS A RESPECTED LITERARY FIGURE WITHIN DENMARK.
OHHHHHH...
...NOW I GET IT!
HE HAD COINED THE TERM "SANDHEDSVIDNE" IN CHRISTIAN DISCOURSES (1848) TO DESCRIBE MARTYRS WHO CAME INTO A FULL UNDERSTANDING OF LIFE THROUGH SUFFERING!

IN EARLIER WORKS, KIERKEGAARD HAD DESCRIBED THE RELIGIOUS STAGE OF LIFE AS THE CULMINATION OF THE THREE STAGES OF DEVELOPMENT OF HUMAN SELF-CONSCIOUSNESS!
HE PERSONIFIED THESE STAGES IN THE CHARACTERS OF DON JUAN, SOCRATES, AND THE WANDERING JEW!
HELLO? TRIPLE-A? THIS IS MYRON EPSTEIN...

...LIKE THE ***BACHELOR*** WHO VOLUNTEERS TO CONSTRICT HIS ***SEXUAL IMPULSES*** BY THE ***ETHICAL CONTRACT*** OF ***MARRIAGE***!

YET THE ETHICAL MAN DISCOVERS THAT OBEYING MORAL LAW BRINGS ***SUFFERING***, SO HE HAS TO MAKE A ***"LEAP OF FAITH"*** (ANOTHER KIERKEGAARD-COINED TERM)...

"THE PARADOX OF FAITH IS *THIS*," KIERKEGAARD WRITES IN *FEAR & TREMBLING* (1843):

"THAT THE INDIVIDUAL IS *HIGHER* THAN THE UNIVERSAL, THAT THE INDIVIDUAL DETERMINES HIS *RELATION* TO THE UNIVERSAL BY HIS RELATION TO THE *ABSOLUTE*."

Individual Universal Absolute

"HE HAS NO NEED OF THOSE EROTIC TINGLINGS IN THE NERVES AT THE SIGHT OF HIS BELOVED ETC., NOR DOES HE NEED TO BE CONSTANTLY TAKING LEAVE OF HER IN A FINITE SENSE..."
"...BECAUSE HE RECOLLECTS HER IN AN ETERNAL SENSE!"

"TO BECOME A CHRISTIAN ACCORDING TO THE NEW TESTAMENT IS TO BECOME 'SPIRIT.'"
"TO BECOME SPIRIT ACCORDING TO THE NEW TESTAMENT IS TO DIE OFF FROM THE WORLD."
"FOR DYING IS FAIRLY BRIEF SUFFERING, WHEREAS DYING OFF LASTS THE WHOLE OF ONE'S LIFE!"

KIERKEGAARD SET ABOUT "DYING OFF FROM THE WORLD" NOT LONG AFTER RECEIVING HIS DOCTORATE IN THEOLOGY IN 1841.
THAT SAME YEAR HE INEXPLICABLY BROKE OFF HIS ENGAGEMENT TO REGINE OLSEN, THE LOVE OF HIS LIFE!

HE REVELED IN HIS ROLE AS A SELF-PROCLAIMED OUTSIDER, AN "EXCEPTION"...
...READING, WRITING, AND THINKING LARGELY IN SOLITUDE IN HIS COPENHAGEN APARTMENT, ALL THE WHILE SUPPORTING HIMSELF ON A SIZEABLE INHERITANCE.

AFTER FLIRTING FOR A TIME WITH HEGELIAN IDEALISM, KIERKEGAARD FOUND AT LAST IN CHRISTIANITY THAT FOR WHICH HE HAD BEEN STRIVING FOR ALL HIS LIFE:
NOW HIRING: IDEAS
"THE THING IS TO FIND A TRUTH WHICH IS TRUE FOR ME, TO FIND THE IDEA FOR WHICH I CAN LIVE AND DIE."

KIERKEGAARD'S WORKS WERE REDISCOVERED BY ACADEMIA IN THE 1950'S, WHEN EXISTENTIALISM WAS ALL THE RAGE. BECAUSE HE'S MORBID AND TALKS ABOUT CHOICES A LOT, MANY REGARD KIERKEGAARD AS "THE FATHER OF EXISTENTIALISM"...
ARE YOU MY DADDY?
VELKOMMEN
...BUT THAT SEEMS TOUGH TO RECONCILE WITH HIS FUNDAMENTALLY RELIGIOUS THINKING:

"A MAN IS BORN IN SIN, ENTERS THIS WORLD BY MEANS OF A CRIME. THE PUNISHMENT-- AND, AS ALWAYS, THE PUNISHMENT FITS THE SIN--"
LIFE
"--THE PUNISHMENT IS TO EXIST."

BUT: "THIS IS WHAT CHRISTIANITY IS FOR--WHICH STRAIGHTAWAY BARS THE WAY TO PROCREATION. THIS MEANS:"
"STOP! I HAVE PUT UP LONG ENOUGH WITH THIS WORLD-HISTORICAL PROCESS."
"CERTAINLY I WILL HAVE PITY, BUT I DO NOT WANT ANY MORE OF THE CONSEQUENCES OF THAT FALSE STEP."

"AND THAT IS WHY CHRISTIANITY UPHOLDS CELIBACY. BY THIS THE CHRISTIAN GIVES CHARACTERISTIC EXPRESSION TO HIS RELATIONSHIP TO THE WORLD...WHICH IS AN OBLIGATION TO STOP IT!"
WE'RE THE LAST MAN AND THE LAST WOMAN ON EARTH, AND NEVER ONCE DID WE MAKE WHOOPIE!
RIP
WHEN WE DIE, HUMANITY ENDS... AND GOD WINS!

"AS A CONSEQUENCE OF CHRISTIANITY, TO LOVE GOD MEANS TO HATE THE WORLD!"
HAD ENOUGH?

FOR KIERKEGAARD, "PRECISELY IN THE SENSE THAT A CHILD PLAYS *SOLDIER* IT IS *PLAYING* AT CHRISTIANITY TO TAKE AWAY THE *DANGER* (CHRISTIANLY, *'WITNESS'* AND 'DANGER' *CORRESPOND*), AND IN ITS PLACE TO INTRODUCE *POWER* ... WORLDLY GOODS, ADVANTAGES, LUXURIOUS ENJOYMENT OF THE MOST EXQUISITE *REFINEMENTS*."

HE WAS ESPECIALLY *GALLED* THAT A WORD OF HIS OWN COINAGE HAD BEEN APPLIED TO A MAN WHOM HE FELT REPRESENTED THE *EXACT OPPOSITE* OF EVERYTHING GOOD AND SPECIAL IN THE CHRISTIAN FAITH!

BETWEEN MAY AND SEPTEMBER 1855 HE BANKROLLED TEN ISSUES OF ØIEBLIKKET ("THE INSTANT"), HIS SELF-PUBLISHED ASSAULT ON THE DANISH CHURCH!
THE INSTANT
THE INSTANT

CENTRAL TO HIS OBJECTIONS WAS THAT CHRISTIANITY WAS A "PRIVATE" RELIGION THAT BECAME BANKRUPTED ONCE INCORPORATED INTO THE ESTABLISHMENT.
CHRISTIAN CLONING MACHINE
HAAAALP! -GLUB!-
HOLY BIBLE
IF PEOPLE COULD BE BORN CHRISTIANS, IT RENDERED THE INDIVIDUAL CHOICE OF "INFINITE RESIGNATION" NOT JUST MEANINGLESS, BUT IMPOSSIBLE!

THOUGH THE INSTANT CAUSED A STIR AT FIRST, MOST DANES GREW TO SEE KIERKEGAARD'S POLEMICS AS REPETITIVE, PETTY BITCHING.
SHOULD WE EXCOMMUNICATE THE NUT?
The Instant
The Instant
WHY BOTHER? IT'S NOT LIKE ANYONE IS LISTENING.

THOUGH HE EXHAUSTED HIS SAVINGS PRODUCING THE INSTANT, REGINE OLSEN REPORTED SHE HAD NEVER SEEN KIERKEGAARD SO HAPPY:
"I FEEL MYSELF REALLY IN MY ELEMENT ONLY WHEN I AM SURROUNDED BY HUMAN MEDIOCRITY AND PALTRINESS!"

HE FELL DEATHLY ILL AT THE BEGINNING OF OCTOBER 1855, AND HAD TO BE HOSPITALIZED. AS HIS CONDITION WORSENED, HE REFUSED COMMUNION UNLESS A LAYMAN, NOT A PRIEST, PERFORMED IT.
"THE CLERGY ARE STATE FUNCTIONARIES, AND FUNCTIONARIES HAVE NOTHING TO DO WITH CHRISTIANITY!"
HE DIED AT 9 AT NIGHT ON NOVEMBER 11.

AT THE FUNERAL, KIERKEGAARD'S ONLY LIVING SIBLING, PETER, HIMSELF A PRIEST, INSISTED THAT THE D.P.C.'S ARCHDEACON TRYDE DELIVER THE COMMITTAL:
MAY GOD HAVE MERCY ON THIS BEWILDERED, PERPLEXED SOUL...
KIERKEGAARD'S NEPHEW HENRIK GREW ANGRIER AND ANGRIER THROUGHOUT THE SERVICE, UNTIL FINALLY:
I MUST PROTEST THE WAY THE CHURCH HAS TREATED MY UNCLE TODAY!
HE DECLARED OFTEN IN HIS WRITINGS THAT HE WAS NOT A CHRISTIAN!
THAT'S A LIE!
YOU KNOW WHAT I MEAN -- THE "AUTOMATIC" KIND OF CHRISTIAN HE DESPISED!
YET THE CHURCH HAS SEIZED HIS BODY--FORCED HIM TO BE COMMITTED TO ETERNITY AS SUCH A CHRISTIAN!
WOULD A RABBI FORCE A CONVERTED JEW TO BE BURIED A JEW? WOULD A TURK (MUSLIM)?
NO, ONLY CHRISTIANS DO THIS! WHAT REVELATIONS SAYS IS TRUE--
--THE STATE CHURCH IS A WHORE SCREWED BY ALL THE TYRANTS OF THE EARTH!
YOU ARE RAPING MY UNCLE'S MEMORY!
STOP THIS THIEF! HE IS DESECRATING HOLY PLACES!
AND SO SOREN KIERKEGAARD HAD THE MOST APPROPRIATE FUNERAL IN HUMAN HISTORY!
I TOLD YOU I'D HAVE THE LAST LAUGH!
HEH, HEH!